Ways & Sounds

Ways & Sounds

Inquiries
Interconnections
Contours

patrick brennan

New York

Ways & Sounds
Copyright ©2021 patrick brennan

All rights reserved. No part of this book may be reproduced or used in any manner without written permission from the author except for the use of quotations in articles or reviews.

ARTEIDOLIA PRESS
P.O. Box 157
New York, N.Y. 10276

Book design: ARTEIDOLIA PRESS
Cover photograph: Randee Silv

arteidolia.com/arteidolia-press

First Edition
Library of Congress Control Number: 2021906886
ISBN: 978-1-7369983-1-1

CONTENTS

Part One: THE STUFF

What is it to Listen ?	1
A Paradox around Identifying "What" Music is	2
What is it that Musicians Do?	4
"Musician" in Three Attitudes	5
Structure, Composition and Sociality	10
Anthropogenic Sound	12
Personics	14

Part Two: STRUCTURES

Composing from the Inside Out	19
Composing from the Outside In	23
Interactive Structure:	
Monological & Dialogical Organization	27
Interactivity	
Monological Structure	
Dialogical Structure	
Rippling Inaudibilities	
Irresolvables	
Notation	38
Metacomposition	46
Metacomposition in Eurological Practice & 4'33"	49
The Jam Session's Metacomposed Interactions	51
Metacomposing the Jam Session	
Links & Foundations	
Adorno's Jam Session Expertise	
Social Philosophy of Polyrhythm	
Repetition, Connection, Continuity	
Metacomposition's "Paltry Stock"	
Provincially Cosmopolitan	
Mycelium to the Forest	

The Garden of Free Improvisation   69
    Blank Boundaries
    How Free is Free?
    Free: Not Easy
    Free Association
Hybrid Strategies: Composing for Improvisers   77
The Conduction Synthesis   84

Part Three: OTHER THOUGHTS

The Electronic Trickster   91
    Musician
    Producer
    Ghosts & Specters
    Flipping the Archival
    Instrument
    Soundscape
The Sociality of Rhythm   123
    God's Eye View
    Microbeats
    Better Behaved Metrics
    Hyperrhythms in Waiting
    Inhabited Rhythm
Hearing   137
& Some Coda Considerations   139

Related Reading   145

Introduction

Most of what transforms sounds into "music" are not the sounds by themselves, but the weave of human activities directed toward those sounds. These include ways of listening, ways of imagining, ways of generating sounds, ways of coordinating people, and ways of conveying information within that process.

When people, especially musicians, talk about "musical structure" they usually mean how the sounds are organized, but there are other structures in play, even more fundamental, that affect our understanding and interpretations of what we hear. These structures are less often spoken of, and more often taken for granted, if thought about at all. What kinds of structures are these? And what are their roles in the "putting together" — in the composing — of a musical event?

This series of essays was written irregularly in chronological sequence between 2011 & 2018 and came to gather themselves into three sections. Part One, *The Stuff*, opens a reexamination of some of the most commonplace language and assumptions regarding music.

What roles are played by listening — or by musicians? Should we restrict our notions of "music" to dictionary definitions such as "a pattern of sounds intended to give pleasure to people listening to it," or should the term *music* more comprehensively denote a complex of sound-focused activities subject to multiple, sometimes contradictory, considerations?

Does the conventional, European derived, paradigm of musical composition, where a single composer designs a fixed, repeatable arrangement of sounds, encompass all possible varieties of compositional action, or might another model help cultivate a more inclusive, more "non-centricized" frame of reference?

How credibly can musical sound be depersonalized, anonymized, disembodied, whether that be through John Cage's more erudite notion of "sounds in themselves" or through the aural carpeting marketplace designation of "music" as an inert consumer object? If we instead recognize person as real and inseparable from musical sound, what would we hear?

Part Two, *Structures*, explores a language regarding composition based in interaction, in the structures of possible social relations among musical participants, and in how musical information, how musical thought, may be communicated while a music is emerging into sound. These together help constitute an ecology of composing. The *act* of composition, the choosing among sounds in the assembling of a sonic image, can be variously situated, each circumstance affording divergent opportunities and circumscriptions. These conditions yield very different sonic events, and each may require distinct recalibrations of recognition, listening and interpretation.

To do this called for repurposing some of our most familiar ways of talking about music, for example, emphasizing "music" and "composing" as, first of all, actions and recasting the noun "composition" as *interactive matrix*. Neologisms such as *dialogical and monological composing, metacomposition* and *personics* were invented to invoke a web of understanding potentially more true to what actually happens in music than do current status quo assumptions about musical structures.

Part Three, *Other Thoughts*, extends from the previous sections to muse over that still recently arrived elephant in the room known as recording, its multiple transformations of our experiences and conceptions of music, as well as a few of the implications of that frequent extrasonic musical actor, rhythm.

These essays evolved cumulatively as a process of discovery, at first simply in order to clarify my own thinking for myself. But, as they evolved, I also recognized that the questions pursued here wouldn't necessarily have to be unique to my particular experience, that other people might likely also be contending with them in their own ways. Here, the adventure approaches possibilities for more public imaginings and discussion, at which point this turns invitation for you to wonder as well.

PART ONE:
The Stuff

1

What is it to Listen?

Sound that proposes music invokes expectancy; and expectancy bathes the possibility of music with the light of attention, with a consent to wait and a willingness to meet. A moment of music accomplishes a tenuous and very fragile consensus within which participants transform what they hear while becoming themselves transformed. A dedication to listening such as this might open a transport into altered states. And conversely, far more than any other predisposition, it's indifference that's most capable of dissolving such gatherings, such doings, as music. When cast beyond the reach of caring, musical sounds disperse into incidental noise.

2

A Paradox around Identifying "What" Music is

Edgard Varèse beautifully defined music as "organized sound;" and people commonly speak of "making" music and of compositions as "pieces" of music, as if "music" were some kind of solid, stable, autonomous object — which it really isn't. Even if a musical recording can be embedded in a tangible media device, as it so often is, the "music" is no such object.

As an action, music engages listening, imagination and sounding. There's a networking of relationships and interactions among perceptions, imaginings, feelings, calculations, sensuosities, social cooperations and techniques. But, without what's ordinarily considered "the music" — which is to say, its sound and *sonic image* — there'd be no musical activity whatsoever. Sound plays to music as do air, wood, water, metal or skin to sound. At the same time, despite this pivotal indispensability, these sounds depend absolutely on the nurturings of musical action in order to exist as music at all.

Music is something that *happens* to sound; and the actions that are *also* music spin themselves around, over and in sounds. Sound harbors musical activity's focal transportation hub. Everything orients toward and through this. Yet, even though actual sounds are so immediately palpable, "the music" isn't residing *exactly* in these "sounds in themselves" (and neither can we do without them). Action, imagination, relationship, all so enmeshed with sound, inseparably and together, collaborate the event we call music.

3

What is it that Musicians Do?

Listeners who aren't generating or sounding music themselves nevertheless *compose* music. In other words, listeners *do* "put music together," as only they themselves can make sense out of the sounds that they hear. To actually invent and initiate musical sound reciprocates by listening out loud.

Musicians serve as advocates for sound entities and their allied silences. They act as liaisons who introduce sounds to expectancy and midwife music into audibility. They work around corners of the heard and the not-heard. They have to listen wide in both directions. They're bound to practice multiple allegiances through having to coordinate the contrasting (and often disparate) interests of sound, craft, imagination, and listeners. Yet, this position doesn't leave that much room for impartiality because musical actions can't become so hypothetical as to turn abstract. They really have to make a difference or they'll just get lost (and if they're not cared about, they aren't going to matter, anyway). Musicians commit to actual sounds and their consequences.

4

"Musician" in Three Attitudes

Amateur — professional — artist…. These clichéd identifiers get thrown around so much that they can distort just as easily as they might clarify. But, even though any cliché tends to sleepwalk its way into stereotype, layering the conventional amateur vs. professional opposition across the relatively anomalous positions that might be dubbed "artist" can begin to map just a few of the attitudes inhabited by a range of musical practitioner.

Musical listening, for example, can be understood as amateur. It's consensual. It's voluntary. And the word amateur itself means "one who loves." Love can't be compelled. And enthusiasm, (which means "having become inhabited by a god") can't be bought either. An amateur attitude reaches as far as pleasure can — and then some. People generate musical sound when they feel like it, and they don't otherwise. Shared enjoyment would best identify the prevailing destination of this mode of relationship. But there are also other relatively unconditional, "gifting" practices of music that reach well beyond these immediate, amateur concerns with a "good time," such as musics that actualize devotion, solidarity or medicinal intent.

In contrast with the consensual communities that can be developed through amateur activity, professional music participates in market relationships that are bounded by "no pay, no play" interactions. These install a firewall between musical practice and the more unconditional loves that move an amateur; and the insulation introduces a wider range of options stretching all the way out into the mercenary.

A professional filter enables the role of musical *fonctionnaire*, where sounds are generated on the basis of external demand. To purvey sounds this way isn't really any less legitimate (or mundane) than any other job; but as a reductionist exercise of professional attitude, it marks where the professional departs most from the motivating concerns of either amateur or artist.

But in general, the impacts of professionalism figure a lot less narrowly and are often much more complicated than this. When music's actually able to attract resources such as income, a demand (as well as an opportunity) evolves for more labor intensive cultivations of craft and capacity that can enlarge everyone's conception of what's possible to achieve musically.

Artists draw on components of both amateur and professional orientations while reaping the contradictions. An artist is a highly intensive amateur who allies the unconditional enthusiasm of the amateur with the discipline and skills applied by professionals (although most of these were probably invented by amateurs and artists in the first place). Amateur and artist may both willingly volunteer their responsibilities toward music; but, while an amateur might regard professional standards of adequacy as an easily disposable option, an artistic disposition aspires instead to invent and contribute well beyond what would ordinarily be standard, passable, adequate or necessary.

Artistic attitude differs most importantly from either professional or amateur in that artists work more for the music than vice versa. And such a potentially exhaustive commitment can wax pretty costly in terms of time, energy and labor. Musicians therefore often turn to the professional sphere not only in order to support themselves (which is a professional value), but to support the music (which poses an artistic one).

But it's pretty difficult to separate these two in practice. Despite that, the differences between professional and artistic attitude aren't really trivial. Push come to shove, the strictly professional has finally to prioritize personal gain over the music itself, whereas an artist chooses to act first as a music's accomplice (with all the problems that might include). And it's not that individual musicians don't change hats all the time just to stay in motion either. It's more a matter of being clear about what's really important in each instance.

Given that plenty of creatively mediocre work can manage to thrive perfectly well in a professional sense, professional activity by itself isn't necessarily a reliable indicator of any music's "quality" or "value" (whatever these words might mean). A lot of serious creative work has long persisted and continues to evolve well off the professional grid without at all qualifying for the sort of dilettantism that such a non-market or "amateur" status might imply.

These attitudes describe a repertoire of roles, different constellations of priorities, rather than fixed personal identities. And whatever conflicts arise among these are even more likely to be lived as individual experiences than they are interpersonally. In practice, actual musicians often inhabit various — even contradictory — amalgams of these alternate fields of intention (any of which might shift on a day to day basis).

The components of whatever mix could as easily support each other as conflict. Amateurs who get paid are suddenly functioning professionally (which might not at all affect how they love what they do). Amateurs or professionals may (or may not) play with the degree of care that derives from artistic attention. The boundaries among these three scales of value are porous and pretty apt to fluctuate.

The spectrum that stretches from amateur to artist begins with an amateur's personal joy in the doing of music (maybe even regardless of how the music sounds). And everyone — absolutely everyone — starts here. The more artistic scale of this spectrum doesn't at all eliminate these joys, but augments them with a growing dedication to the welfare and life of music's sound in a way that develops beyond personal indulgence into a reciprocal dialogue and responsibility. Professional activity offers a vehicle capable of either supporting or abusing what's achieved along this spectrum — as well as delivering varying mixtures of both at the same time.

• • •

The presence (or prospect) of a listener — the pressure and pull of that focused waiting that could be called expectancy — activates a musical arena with restless, destabilizing, gravitational currents that each sound has to address upon entering into music. Neutrality's not an available option. Musical sounds assert amid uncertainties that always promise opportunities for failures. They have to dance among vagaries of attention, among she-loves-me-she-loves-me-nots, among with-its and not-with-its, among persuasion, seduction, resistance, distraction, defiance. Worlds are already in motion. Sounds already present their own character. So do listeners. There isn't any blank slate from which a musician may begin.

Even a musician who happens to be composing in isolation at a particular moment is therefore never really alone or asocial, working "only for oneself," because, as a community language and project, music's mode of address is a constitutionally convivial and public one. Musicians inevitably engage beyond "self" in their responsibilities to the sound entities and unsounded motions with whom they're collaborating. This fulfills a symbiotic partnership that furthers music's evolution and continuing subsistence.

5

Structure, Composition and Sociality

A commonplace in some discussions about music concerns whether a particular instance of music is "structured" or "unstructured." This is a distinction that seems to assume that it's not really all that unusual to encounter events that have no structure whatsoever (which might just be pushing it a bit). It would seem that anything we run into (and not just music) would occasion some sort of structure, even if that "structure" may seem anomalous. But, rather than quibbling over a presence or absence of "structure" in any music, why not ask questions about what kind of structures are coming into play or about what purposes a particular structural arrangement might facilitate?

Usually when people talk about "structure" in music, they're referring only to relationships among sounds; they're talking about sonic design, which is no trivial concern among musicians. But there are other important structures that deeply affect and qualify a sonic image in music. These are the structures of cooperation and communication among the people who generate the sound.

Likewise, the word *composition* in music talk usually refers only to sonic organization, but a lot more has to be composed than *sonic* relationships. Something of a body politic has also to be composed for *any* music to happen. People have to agree to cooperate. Communication strategies and methods of coordination have to be worked out. All of this together assembles a musical structure. Musical composition's organization is social as much as it is sonic.

Any musical composition enlists a *social* agreement in order to achieve its sound. A working consensus gathers around which sounds are to be recognized as "the music" along with how people are to coordinate with each other while generating these sounds. Each specific composition focuses the constitution of an equally specific (if provisional) sonic community.

6

Anthropogenic Sound

In putting sounds together, in *composing*, a composer makes decisions about which sounds go where and when they go there. This is what a composer does — and *anybody* (that means *anybody*) who does this is composing. What distinguishes a musician's composing from a listener's is that a musician's constructions turn audible.

Most musical bodies of sound manage to self-identify as "music." A listener doesn't have to *like* a sound or even accept it as "music" *for oneself*, just acknowledge that it's got to somehow qualify as "music" for *somebody*. Somewhat less often are there sonic events (such as many of those fostered by John Cage, for example) that, rather than quite so explicitly identifying themselves as a sonic exception that could only indicate music, have often to lean instead on institutional brackets to be introduced to musical attention. But, generally a listener usually doesn't have to wonder too much *whether* some sounds are "music" or not because a musical sound body messages a distinctively social gesture that invites a listener to engage it face to face. It invites a listener *to compose along with it*.

Musical sound might so engross a listener that many may rarely ever move their considerations beyond what a particular music can do *for them* (and how could anybody really enjoy listening without some occasion for self gratification anyhow?). But a musical sound some occasion for self gratification anyhow?). But a musical sound body's very capacity to "self identify" derives from other avenues of access it presents. Not so different from the way the shifting geometries of beach sand recount patterned motions of wind and water, musical sounds distinctively symptomize *human* activity; and this is why it so often draws the turns of the head that it does. Some*body*'s doing something. *People* are doing something. What's up? An alert uncertainty edging on wariness begins to tone attention, and for good reason too: any living system (and people especially) behaves just unpredictably enough to bear some watching out for. Musical sounds consequently always pose news.

Sounds point back to their generating frictions. And the sound of a human generated event points even farther back toward the people who've initiated these sounds. A telltale *whoness* insinuates among sound's acutely sensorial *whatness*. Sonic images swell with forensic clues that both imply and trace the decision streams of their composers.

An overall sound may impart ambience, *feel*, tone, perhaps even mood; but the compositional choices marking and distinguishing a sound body are what deliver a music's *drama*. Imaginative, empathic, even speculative attention to the impacts of agency on musical sound can reach toward prospective "whys" *behind* sounds and into the inhabitable "what ifs" of music's sonic fiction, wherein one might infer — and *feel* — the sensibilities and dispositions of minds (or even states of mind) other than one's own.

7

Personics

Persona offers a beautiful and evocative word. An off the cuff guess as to its etymology might associate *per* (for) with *sona* (or *son*) as "sound," thus *per-sona* meaning "for sound." But, apparently this isn't the case. The word *persona* circulated among the Etruscans of ancient Italy to designate a mask spoken through by an actor during theatrical performances. A notion of mask implies vehicle or point of transfer, while the word *persona* itself recalls its kindred terms, such as *personage, personality, person, personal.*

A *sonic persona* constitutes a composer's audible mask. It's an identity — as protagonistic as in theatre — that articulates an image of agent or actor; and it accomplishes this through neither words, gesture nor facial expression, but conjures this impression instead out of no more than sound alone. Persona sounds the tip of a composer's index finger: Listen here! Listen to this! Listen! It articulates its presence through achieving a distinctive way of assembling sound, a pattern and flavor of compositional choices that establish a cumulatively recognizable identity.

Relatively stable sonic imagery that's been collaboratively invented and maintained bit by bit by many contributors over time exerts more of a *community* persona, but this presents a persona nevertheless. No one person in particular may be responsible for the music's design, but regardless of this, the music has *still* been composed, and its sound chronicles as much discerning and preferring as would any other. Likewise, interpretive performers, musicians whose choices supplement a predetermined sonic image, compose to the extent that their decisions modulate the quality and presence of the music they're playing; and as with actors, there's enough discretionary latitude in interpretation that many inspiring performers achieve uniquely identifiable personae of their own.

Where an interpretive performer cultivates persona through execution, a composer effects persona more through musical design, through choice of patterns and patterns of choice. Sonic imagery doesn't self generate, nor is it self-sustaining. It has always to be built, constructed, *put together*, composed. Options have to be considered. Decisions have to be made. There are uncertainties — and there grows an ongoing dialogue with conditions. What becomes audible from all this is not necessarily autobiography or self expression (however powerfully each composer's peculiar affinities inevitably color these events). What insinuates among the sounds is the relationships of all of these protagonists in interaction.

Individuals, however, are not at all disposable options. The resonance of the individual person that emerges in music derives from the topographical specificity and uniqueness of the intersection where that particular human being is happening. The irregular, the unpredictable, the anomalous, the capacity to recognize, sort and integrate the random and surprise, the generative sources of new life in music originate, as elsewhere, with microcosmic *individual* exceptions to statistical averages. The sounds that speak as an exception, as *music*, display an accrual of these individual divergences. Musical sound resonates as distinctly *personified* sound.

PART TWO:
Structures

8

Composing from the Inside Out

The conventional demarcations maintained between composition and improvisation are fake ones; or, to put it just a bit more generously, they're at the very least more than a little misleading; Allegations that improvisers *don't* compose only imposes more unnecessary and distracting confusion. The distinctions addressed here don't actually relate to the *act* of composing itself (choosing among sounds in the assembling of a sonic image is what musicians are doing in either setting). A differentiation that really does matter, however, concerns *how* the activity of composing is situated.

Steve Lacy deftly contrasted these options in precisely 15 seconds:

> In 15 seconds, the difference between composition and improvisation is that in composition you have all the time you want to decide what you want to say in 15 seconds, while in improvisation you have 15 seconds.

The cosmology within which a composer acts, the terms of action, the kinds of information available, the relationship with the sonic image, all differ radically, but musicians might easily snap from one end of this spectrum to the other just like that; and they're additionally apt to organize a plethora of mixed strategies in relation with what it is they want to accomplish.

Improvisation is not a complete misnomer for situating the compositional process within sonic events as they unfold. A composer has to integrate responses and anticipations toward what's *imprevisto*, toward what's *unforeseen*, as a given feature of the field of action. A composer here weaves coherences amid an *open* system. In physicist Ilya Prigogine's notion of *dissipative structures*, the more coherent, the more interconnected an open system (and, in the case of music, the more communications effected), the more *unstable* it is — the more capable of (or liable to) sudden transformations. Under these conditions, as the poet Charles Olson also relates in his essay *Projective Verse*:

> ONE PERCEPTION MUST IMMEDIATELY AND DIRECTLY LEAD TO A FURTHER PERCEPTION. ... keep moving, keep in, speed, the nerves, their speed, the perceptions, theirs, the acts, the split second acts, the whole business, keep it moving as fast as you can, citizen.

Compositional immersion in the quick of the moment affords intimate access to, and direct rapport with, the fine local details of the actual sounds at hand — timing, timbre, envelope, emphasis — vital details of affective touch that can move deeply a listener's attention, and which, taken all together, would be, in practical terms, simply too intricate to either average, map or delegate.

What comes along with such compositional intimacy is a necessity to respond inventively to whatever unannounced shifts happen to permeate a musical biosphere. The fluctuating sonic imagery that's so characteristic of music being composed in this way demonstrates the telling impact of the call and response exchanges that are so intrinsic to how open systems interact with their environment.

Improvisation as *attitude* — as an open system, give and take cosmology — as an *ethos*, relates (not so surprisingly) with a lot more than *musical* activity. Albert Murray writes in *The Hero and the Blues* that

> Improvisation is the ultimate human (i.e. heroic) endowment. It is, indeed; and even as flexibility or the ability to swing (or to perform with grace under pressure) is the key to that unique confidence which generates the self-reliance and thus the charisma of the hero, and even as infinite alertness-become-dexterity is the functional source of the magic of all master craftsmen, so may skill in the art of improvisation be that which both will enable contemporary man to be at home with his sometimes tolerable but never quite certain condition of not being at home in the world and will also dispose him to regard his obstacles and frustrations as well as his achievements in terms of adventure and romance.

But, from the point of view of crafting an audible sonic image that's faithful to an imagined one, improvisation also freights a good share of inconveniences, liabilities and lacks. Improvisers may willingly choose to compose within acutely abrupt horizons; but in having situated themselves *inside* (rather than outside) a musical event, composers can only act from where they actually are at any moment, at most passingly with the beginning of an event and only briefly with its end along the way. Musical information continues to shift throughout, perpetually contingent and imperfect. A profound *influence* might be effected through adroit blendings of cooperation and counterstatement, but any *total* control over a global sonic narrative is simply not in the cards for any participant — and it can't be. Accurate knowledge of an evolving and still indeterminate soundscape can never be more than provisional and speculative. These are the both limiting and liberating conditions that shape the context and basis within which instantaneous musical invention asserts itself.

Completely out in the open, improvisation radically exposes compositional process and ensconces it without retroactive safety nets within a series of irreversible actions and commitments. Coherence and presence have to be achieved adaptively and cumulatively. And the debris of improvised music's construction — its scaffolds, its hesitations, mistakes, digressions, experiments and reassessments — splays openly within unforgiving earshot. All of this, together with the composers' responses, assembles what narratives greet a listener.

The doubts intrinsic to improvisation, its continual spar and dance with approaching vortices of unresolved probabilities enact a drama immediately inhabitable by listeners and composers alike in a way that all can share a stake in the outcome. This shared intensification of expectancy can become a collective achievement. And, given its dicey, if not occasionally adverse, circumstances, it's not all that surprising that persuasive composing from-the-inside-out smacks so much of miracle and revelation for both listener and composer in a way that vividly immerses all participants in the suspense and dynamism of creative process.

9

Composing from the Outside In

Composing a sonic image from the outside in de-synchronizes compositional choices and their sounding by segmenting musical generation into two discrete stages: that of composition and *performance*. This is a strategic reorganizational scheme that affords composers some respite from the unmitigated rush of living soundstreams. To abstract compositional choice *away* from performance in this way can grant composers a greater degree of repose, some time to think, reconsider, edit, refine and clean up — and all of this, well *before* committing finally to sound.

This staggered division of labor also introduces a capacity to expedite compositional control at a scale and precision that's unattainable through ensemble improvisation. More exacting correspondences between an imagined sonic ideal and its actualization in sound can be drawn within a composer's reach. But, in order to hold sounds so accountable to a composer's ideal, their sonic image has also to stabilize. Sounds and patterns must regularize and turn more dependably repeatable. They depart from the changeable volatility of "event" into an emulation of what Amiri Baraka has disparagingly termed "artifact."

Outside-in composing applies closed system dynamics in generating sonic imagery. Sound bodies are conceived as finite quantities to be measured, divided up and ordered accordingly (and to limit variables in this way furthermore aids in optimizing compositional control). This may offer one possible explanation as to why divisive structures, internal formal consistency and linear development from clear beginning to definite end have so come to predominate as indicators of appropriate and successful compositional practice for some.

Actual sound bodies fade as immediate environs for compositional choice and assume a new role as its terminal destination. Sounds are cast as objects of observation, poised distant within a regard roughly analogous with a European Renaissance painter's methodical launching of illustrated objects toward vanishing points. In a curious inversion of the English art historian Walter Pater's 19th century suggestion, this system of organizing musical composition poses an instance of musical practice aspiring to the conditions of visual art.

Sound's indigenous ephemerality, however, slips aside the relative endurance of sculpted stone or fresco. In contrast with the ever so tangible, but potent, "leftover" that's called "art object," musical sound isn't freestanding or "autonomous" in this way, but perpetually dependent on its enactment in performance. However, if so desired, what might best approximate the hardscapes of visual artifact could be a recourse to repetition on a grand scale, a firm commitment to thorough *re*-enactment, to an acting out the *ideal* of the artifact, the "unchanging" object, as *ritual* (which, in contrast with *play*, would filter out unanticipated creative intrusions in advance).

When carefully deployed, outside-in strategies are able to yield sonic imagery of airbrushed, nearly hyperreal perfection, but such an achievement by itself doesn't really represent some kind of apotheosis of musical possibility. It articulates only one alternate proportioning of the complex tradeoffs negotiated among the conflicting interests of imagination, social organization and sound. In this particular variety, performance is rendered as much commemoration as realization.

As with belated news of a long expired supernova, music's generative compositional energy has been exiled to a remote, possibly forgettable (and even disposable) historical resting place. The tensions among the inconclusive, the tentative and the decisive have long since transpired way off in some yesterday, to leave behind some potentially vivid, but unavoidably second hand news.

Nevertheless, a music's sound and design may still (and often does) profoundly move a listener, but only along a one way street along which the music can neither move itself, hear or respond. And conversely, beyond the narrowed options of dissent, disruption or displacement, neither listener nor performer may move the music either. This is musical "composition" posed as sonic monument.

In the 21st century, where automated repetition has turned so cheap and easy, it could seem hard to imagine that the archival taint that can now be so easily associated with current, Eurological (an apt term, along with *Afrological*, developed by George Lewis) "classical" practice, for example, might be persisting as an unintended consequence of what was, at the time of its earlier development, cutting edge innovation. Living without high technologies for capturing and preserving sonic imagery, the fixed, replicable complex sonic patterns invented and developed by earlier European composers were most likely encountered as exceptional achievements amid a much more tenuously evanescent sonic world.

Not only did many of these composers improvise (even if that procedure *was* restricted to solo execution), their actual working conditions fared a good deal closer to Duke Ellington's than to, say, Pierre Boulez (and in more ways than class and status). Like Ellington, they were expected to constantly produce new material. One's "best" piece really did have to be one's *next* piece. They were way too busy looking ahead to be thinking in terms of bequeathing cryonic deposits for a future museum status.

All tradeoffs aside however, closed system composing allows a development of ideas and sound bodies that's can't be arrived at through open systems. And there are many kinds of sonic images that can *only* be constructed through this kind of framework. Some music can only be discovered from the inside out. Other sonic imaginings can only be achieved through highly intensive planning and scripting. Each specific conception has to appeal to whatever its most supportive methodology turns out to be. In a pluralistic musical world, where no particular musical *way* can carry a last word, outside-in composing distinguishes itself as a very frequently visited and especially useful station along the sonic pathways.

10

Interactive Structure: Monological & Dialogical Organization

Interactivity

Who decides influences compositional structure the most. A music's *interactive structure* adapts accordingly — with a corresponding impact on the music's *sonic image* (this is the audible portion of the music that a listener hears). Interactive structure coordinates the flow of *musical information* within an ensemble; and *musical information* indicates which sounds happen when. A compositional structure orients the areas of convergence and divergence around which an ensemble organizes itself.

These structures gather toward two basic configurations. If a music's sonic image derives from the decisions of a *single* composer, its interactive structure could be called *monological.* If a sound body accommodates the interchanges of *more than one* composer, its interactive structure could be understood as a *dialogical* one. The two alternatives organize very different varieties of musical performance, while a range of differently proportioned mixed structures are able to blend these in a variety of ways.

Monological Structure

During a storyteller's monologue, any variety of guises, disguises, ruses, voices or masks may be donned in the telling. A monologist can deftly dissolve behind the specter of tale; but what keeps this event *monologue* is that it's *not* interrupted. The story emits from a solitary agent. The relative dearth of interactive information in monological performance minimizes ensemble response and initiative in deference to the clarity of this single compositional signal. There's little doubt invited as to the responsible source of the music's sonic design.

Within a monologically organized interactive structure, performers coordinate around the directives of a single *compositional persona*. This *persona* may speak for one actual person (or "composer"). It may assemble the composite persona of an advance collaboration of contributors. It may represent an inherited, collective, anonymous or "traditional" persona (or it may be posed as an otherwise adopted model for imitation). Whatever the actual source, it's this compositional persona who's decided *which sounds happen when*.

Within a monological structure, musical information flows unidirectionally along a lineal, cause-and-effect sequence from "composer" (or model), to performer, to listener. The steady reference signal of a designated sonic image is collectively accepted as non-negotiable and is bounded clearly by "right notes" and "wrong notes."

By definition, then, performers of monological music absolutely *do not* decide which sounds happen; and in this sense, they most emphatically *do not* compose (although unavoidable gaps in any set of instructions always grant some latitude for interpretation). Performers must listen for a composer's designated sonic image while they listen closely to each other in order to assure that it's being achieved in accurate tandem. Such careful uncertainty amid swift proximity to breakdown animates some of the essential tensions and heroism of musical performance.

Streamlining a music's interactive structure this way helps establish a fairly unambiguous field of reference for ensemble convergence and divergence that collaterally frees each performer to concentrate ever more carefully on individual details of application. *Convergence* assembles around appropriate and well coordinated execution, while *divergence* can only register as *mistake*.

Monological composers precipice the apex of a closed, command and control system. However efficient this may be for a number of purposes, the literal remoteness of such a "remote control" system almost too easily exposes compositional directives to potential sabotage, carelessness, incompetence or sullen compliance — with the composer (well, at least a *living* composer) being the most likely to reap whatever blame there is to be had for the resulting sound.

The trust that links a monological composer's conceptions with its executors holds perennially fragile. One important response to this has been to rigorously standardize musicianship so that instrumentalists sound so nearly identical that they can achieve a sort of anonymous interchangeability (as is the case in Euroclassical training). There are some very good reasons for this too. A thoroughgoing regularization helps insure that composers who design for particular instruments actually have a prayer of hearing what they've mapped out.

Standardization, however, can also ricochet back toward composers at a great expense to sound and conception. Not only has many an "individualist" composer become heard only at the mercy of rigorous conventionalization, but many musical conceptions have had to be adapted to conventional terms and their accompanying social milieus.

Some avant-garde composers have attempted to break through this sort of impasse with a nearly unbearable weight of compensatory, micromanaged specification; but this also carries with it a downside that ever smaller communities of musicians may become able and willing to sound that music. And yet another progressively more available — and ever more popular — response to this dilemma has been to dispense with people altogether and offload this entire problem of musical transmission onto machinery.

Dialogical Structure

Within dialogical conditions, composers fare no less vulnerable to missteps and disruptions of collaborators than in monological settings. However, where a plurality of contributors simultaneously venture compositional choices, it's also mutually recognized that individual decision streams will begin immediately to diverge. This centrifugal tension fuels and complements ongoing and collective renegotiations of the music's convergences.

Within dialogical structures, compositional information flows multidirectionally. Interactions are complex, reciprocal and, in exact detail, unpredictable. Initiatives are continually absorbed, reevaluated and transformed from as many different perspectives as there are contributors.

Direct compositional control withdraws to within the reach of each composer's own instruments and sonic initiatives. When each assumes direct responsibility for sound generation as a performer, an ensemble coalition can be assembled with a lot less recourse to individual standardization. A platform thus opens the sonic palette to idiosyncratic knowledge and capacity, to the one of a kind, the untamable, the unmappable, the unusual and the unanticipated.

A dialogical composer, therefore, willingly foregoes monological responsibilities to positions of omniscience for an opportunity to intervene directly in music's finding shape as it happens, to be able to change one's mind — and to do this while in collaborative interchange with minds and sensibilities that are *not* one's own.

Exchanging monological control over a music's global sonic image for *relationship*, each participates in a more decentralized creative project, within which a network of connections is composed — and, it's this slightly transpersonal collective network that's actually composing the music.

Alert to personal imagination, ensemble coordination and the evolving sonic image, dialogical composers *listen to each other in order to decide what to play next.* Overall coherence develops as each participant draws (and draws upon) opportune connections among the sonic initiatives of one's compatriots.

Sounds, patterns and concepts (a.k.a. musical "material") assume an additional function alongside articulating a sonic image: they simultaneously *communicate* musical information among participating composers. Structural communication is thus audibly *externalized* (rather than hidden as in monological formats) *through* the sounds of the music. This allows composers to "talk to" each other while the very same sounds are also addressing their audience. The composite sonic image of all of these interchanges reflects necessary feedback for continuing inventions and interventions.

Within such a network, dialogical gestures also become structurally *provocative*, angled not only *to sound*, but also to evoke *response* elsewhere in the flow of the music. A volatile give and take ripples among the various decision streams that are generating the music. A silence can accent ongoings in an ensemble just as powerfully as any flurry. What counts is the relationship with context, placement, timing and the total synergy of interactions. It's not for nothing that Miles Davis practiced boxing from a specifically *musical* perspective.

Rippling Inaudibilities

There isn't really any one-size-fits-all rubric for relating with musical sound as if it were born ziplessly out of some miracle of immaculate conception. A music can't be fully recognized without dedicating some attention toward its inaudibilities.

What is it in music that might be *inaudible*? Silence, for example, can be acutely *audible*; but dance as a component of a music, beyond explicitly percussive contributions, is, for the most part, not. Attention itself stays inaudible — as do imagination, consideration, decision and coordination. All may become evident *through* sound. The invisible might turn corporeal while audibly dressed.

The *activity* that is music isn't so much literally heard as *inferred* through relationship *with* sound and through relationships *among* sounds. The social structure of musical generation (which includes *who* decides *what* — *when*, *where* and *how* decisions are enacted —

how this information circulates within an ensemble — and *how* they achieve sound) constitutes an indispensable, however unsounded, component of a music's *composition,* of *how it's put together.*

The choices that are composition deposit traceable pathways amid a musical sound body. To listen to a music is also to follow where its composers are going, and the drama one might witness has to vary with circumstances. To judge composition in one context by the constraints, standards & possibilities of another is to purchase a swift ticket to unnecessary confusion and misapprehension.

A monological format reveals the "thinking" of one compositional persona, while dialogical settings present the multiple contentions of a plurality of musical "thinkers." One assays the challenge of internal or personal congruence while the other communally refracts this same endeavor within a conversation of perspectives.

Where monological coordination leans deterministic, dialogical structures bend probabilistic. One optimizes the clarifying advantages of stasis, while the other calibrates *homeostasis.* With the exception of *a cappella* solo improvisation, monological organization aspires toward replicable, stable sonic imagery, while sonic images of dialogical music fluctuate in accordance with the curvature of its compositional interactions.

Monological methods don't so much "solve," once and for all, the challenges of structural communication and coordination in music as try to eliminate them through a somewhat Fordist standardization that narrows ensemble interaction to its lowest possible minimum. Interaction is kept so much the same every time that, regardless of the music sounded, it seems to disappear almost entirely as an element of musical structure.

Contrastingly, the acute interdependency of collaborating composers in dialogical music renders interaction and relationship central and indispensable components of musical composition. The efficiency and success of monological organization relies on just one single species of social cooperation, while the possible configurations of interactive coordination figure more than can be counted.

Irresolvables

Social organization can't really be ostracized as either a core element of musical composition or as an important component of a music's total aesthetic statement. The momentum and impact of the social in musical composition, far beyond instrumental mechanics of how sounds are generated, has been insightfully assessed by Christopher Small in his *Music of the Common Tongue*:

> We are moved by music because musicking creates the public image of our most inwardly desired relationships, not just showing them to us as they might be but actually bringing them into existence for the duration of the performance. This will clearly involve our deepest feelings, and thus the act of musicking, taking place over a duration of time, teaches us what we really feel about ourselves and about our relationships to other people and to the world in general, helping us to structure those feelings and therefore to explore and evolve our own identity.... 'How do I know what I feel until I hear what I play?' In musicking, in fact we are being touched in the deepest parts of who we are.

The gaps between music imagined, music sounded and music heard nest composers in imperfectly resolvable, aesthetic and ethical conflicts of interest. What's more important — the sound or the way people interrelate? What's more valuable — a relatively egalitarian distributing of individual initiative and interaction, or a single individual assuming centralized command? Is musical activity simply a technical means to a sonic end, or is the sound an indicative partner of the activity? What kind of world, developed through what kind of relationships, is worth cultivating?

These are social questions, questions of worldview, questions about a conception of the human, cosmological questions that don't actually separate from decisions about sounds. Social and sonic imagination aren't automatically fit to each other in advance at all; and it might even be supposed that sounds likewise have their own (possibly quite contrary) social notions.

Composers can't completely avoid at least implicitly taking a stand on these considerations. Every time one composes, a social position is declared, or at the minimum, explored. And, at the same time, those not-yet-heard sonic entities for which composers are responsible might be demanding social coordination appropriate to *their* needs irrespective of social vision.

There's no "perfect" solution. Monological music aspires for the most part to a stable sonic image that corresponds accurately with sonic imagination. Sonic images are frozen at the cost of interactive motility on behalf of a reliable clarity and precision. To keep an image stable and consistent, performers can't afford to move out of line. They can't comment on the music. They can't talk back. They can neither add to the music nor extend it. Interactive aspects of music are kept as dead, comatose or suspended as possible. The social structure is hierarchical and command based.

Bypassing direct human collaboration (and interference) — as do electronic studio, computer or otherwise generated sound — no less declares an attitude toward musical social interaction than does live music. In absenting performers, this presents something of a post neutron bomb soundscape. It's for the most part, no *less* monological: but it *is* less hierarchical — if only because there are no longer any people involved in the music's generation process to be issuing commands to.

In multipersonic, interactive composition (a.k.a. collective improvisation), as composers move, so does sound. A clear fidelity to an individually imagined overall sound runs fugitive because an improvising ensemble's sonic image simply *can't* stand still. Communication among compositional personae can't be hidden. All of which displays some of the apparent "messiness" that horticultural forest gardening tends to show when compared with the surface tidiness of industrial agriculture — until one begins to consider all the internal connections that are (or aren't) going on. There's a trade off in that monological organization hardly allows at all for recomposing interaction, whereas dialogical structures open to a musical composition of interaction and relationship itself. This is yet something else to listen for.

While there may be an undeniably long history of *solo* improvisation within Europe's formalized tradition, no situation has developed *dialogical* composition with the depth and thoroughness that African Americans have while navigating the dreams, myths and contradictions of life in the United States. Parallel with the still deferred, expansively inclusionist vision pursued under Radical Reconstruction, people who have themselves directly witnessed and experienced being forcibly classified as inert objects, as property, as criminal (which is to say "escaped" property) or otherwise somehow less than human, brilliantly evolved under these conditions of almost perpetually compromised safety a musical methodology that communicates sonic coherence while nurturing and facilitating the individual agency of each participant, a model not only socially restorative and viable, but one more consistent with the expansion of knowledge in biology and physics (and this, by the way, isn't at all to say that quantitative sciences should be determining any art) than the structural consolidations inherited from 19th century Europe.

Neither dialogical nor monological organization by itself at all guarantees "good" or "better" music. Their dissimilarities are so location specific that comparisons of their interactive topographies can't really say anything about the "quality" of a music being generated (which emerges instead out of how composers might *navigate* a particular terrain). Neither can be "superior" to the other because they're responding to different concerns. And no one concern, whether sonic or interactive integrity, holds superior to any other either — but they *are* different; and these are distinctions decisively crucial for both composing and listening.

There are yet other ways of imagining relationships among these alternatives. One would be to consider the speed of a composition's evolution. Some ideas evolve instantaneously. Others molt and transform themselves very gradually — and do so slowly enough to be exhaustively mapped. The movement and change between a series of "frozen" monological compositions might portray a very different process than would any one of them in isolation. The mutual influence and responsiveness of monological composers to each other shows a much slower kind of dialogue (even if not a part of performance) than does collective improvisation. A composer's ensemble might even be structured where each participant alternately takes turn in composing for the others. Then, there's also composing *for* improvisers. This opens a whole other spectrum of possibilities — and a very, very important one.

Unlike an individual plant, animals aren't bound to a single location. A composer can go monological on Sunday, dialogical all day Monday and mix it all up on Tuesday. Sometimes the sonic image gets some; sometimes the interaction does. Sometimes they talk to each other and work it out for a while. Every moment, every position in the spectrum *says* something, *means* something. At least, none of them are *neutral*.

11

Notation

The limits of communication in any particular situation define the possible topographies of a musical event. In order to sound a sonic image (whether predetermined or articulated in progress) a sonic community organizes its activities around the musical information that's cuing *which sounds happen when*. It's this communication of information that animates the circulatory and nervous systems of a music. What can be circulated, and therefore sounded, is constrained within the horizons of human capacity. These horizons curve along the thresholds of memory, attention, interpretive capability, reflexes, ingenuity, habit, adaptability, intuition, technical facility and the generalizing and classification systems (whether personal or collective) that synthesize masses of musical information into manageable bunches.

Notation — the visual mapping of sonic patterns (especially as developed in Europe since that region's Middle Ages) — hosts an extraordinary prosthetic extension of memory that accomplishes a remarkably far reaching messaging system. Its impact on musicking, on conceptualizations of music and on musical imagination is notably formidable.

Long before synthesizers and digital quantization, notation codified abstractions of actual sound to a visual, legible and transportable system. The now familiar, descriptive variables applied in musical notation include graphic representations of differences in pitch frequency (metaphorically depicted as "high" and "low" — in place of, say, *faster/slower, thinner/thicker* or *smaller/larger*), along with the sequential passage of sonic events plotted horizontally from left to right (as European languages are also written). This mapping of "time" is further simplified into proportional, sequential bits. "Time" is segmented into progressive steps out of which are derived measures, meters and note values such as half-note, quarter-note, and so forth. Notation, however, offers more than just a tool. The nature of its specifications articulates an editorially selective point of view regarding both sound and music.

The French sociologist of science, Bruno Latour, in a paper entitled *Drawing and Cognition: Drawing Things Together,* considered the impact of perspective drawing and mapmaking in some ways that could be compared with notation's relationship with music. The development of a homogeneous language based in longitude, latitude and geometry, permitted the spatial relationships among components of an area of land (or, say, a building) to be fixed in a notated form that could travel and make that depicted location persuasively visible (or in the case of building, even replicable) to people in places far away. Not only that, fictitious imaginings, whether hybrid fantasy or the design of a hypothetical machine, could be accessibly presented through these same media tools as "real."

Latour notes that:

> Papers and signs are incredibly weak and fragile. This is why explaining anything with them seemed ludicrous at first. La Perouse's map is not the Pacific anymore than Watt's drawings and patents are engines, or the bankers' exchange rates are the economies, or the theorems of topology are "the real world". This is precisely the paradox. By working on papers alone, on fragile inscriptions which are immensely less than the things from which they are extracted, it is still possible to dominate all things and all people. What is insignificant for all other cultures becomes the most significant, the only signifi-

cant aspect of reality. The weakest, by manipulating inscriptions of all sorts obsessively and exclusively, become the strongest.

Latour also points out that:

> Inscriptions are made flat. There is nothing you can dominate as easily as a 'flat surface of a few square meters; there is nothing hidden or convoluted, no shadows, no "double entendre". In politics as in science, when someone is said to "master" a question or to "dominate" a subject, you should normally look for the flat surface that enables mastery (a map, a list, a file, a census, the wall of a gallery, a card-index, a repertory); and you will find it.

Just a few square meters of musical notation can enable a monological composer to design the construction of, for example, a four hour long sonic event that involves the coordination of over a hundred people — and to designate all of this in extremely fine detail. The labyrinthine, even perplexing, passing by of actual sounds and patterns become shadow frozen, somewhat like Eadweard Muybridge's early photographic motion studies. Patterns can be arrested, investigated, reexamined and refined still further. Notation in this way poses a sonic parallel with the drafter's camera obscura.

However, unlike the receptive depiction of physical objects and their relations in space relative to an observer, notation assertively reverses the exchange. The abject weakness of an abandoned, unread sheet of score paper exposes a vital necessity that notation position itself as an irresistible and overwhelming social magnet in order to wax viable at all. With the consensual amiability of sympathetic magic, notation introduces into the social relations of music a binding written contract that opportunes to dictate what is and isn't "music" in terms of its own peculiar limits and possibilities.

As tails wag dogs, musical notation shapes an entire sonic community around its requirements (and without an accommodating social network, notation can't hold sway). Participants must "feed the medium" through acquiring a fluency in its codes; and an entire educational culture (a sort of bureau of weights and measures) has to develop to safeguard consistent and accurate correspondences between written description and sonic execution. With all the commitment required to make notation practicable, it's not so surprising that, in some circles, notated music comes to represent the very definition of "music" — period — with notation posing as border guard between composer and performer in a monological division of labor.

The tactical advantages of socially supported notation are nevertheless pretty hard to dismiss. Its immense storage capacity can compensate for human cognitive limits in some remarkable ways. The perspective stillness of paper can imaginarily "stop time." A composer can step aside from the pressures of sonic immediacy and inhabit instead a niche a lot closer to that of a studio artist or a novelist than to an active performer. The reflective calm and isolation of paper (or electronic studio) composing favors an uninterrupted focal concentration that can be refreshed by walking away without worries that the preserved sonic patterns might dissolve, disappear or be forgotten (direct, live composing, in contrast, enjoys little to none of this luxury). The archeological endurance of notation is even capable of withstanding the absence of a composer due to death. As long as the cultural practices of decoding persist, a notated sonic pattern can be resuscitated over and over, regardless.

Many of the unique inventions developed by European composers over centuries that have importantly contributed to the world's musical inheritance may not have developed at all without the complicity of notation. Early European notation may have first memorized, preserved and conveyed the already existing, unadorned, monophonic, text related, melodic shapes of Gregorian chant; but it's hard to conceive how the Late Medieval Flemish composers or the Ars Nova could have constructed their complex polyphonies without detailed architectural sketches and renderings (and it may not be so coincidental that these intensely architectonic constructions were themselves designed for sounding within the cathedral acmes of that era's architecture.). Counterpoint, fugue, diatonic tonality, and Schoenberg's pantonality are all complex generative techniques whose development required detailed trial and error comparison on par with that of a mathematician or physicist. As Latour might argue, careful comparison of documentation is key to weeding out inconsistencies in the construction of a system.

Within an interactive structure that channels most musical information by way of the page, not only does the eye vie for predominance over the ear, but, where paper comes to do most compositional "thinking," performers actually *don't have to*. It may seem paradoxical, but diminishing a performer's compositional responsibility allows more elaborate and dense musical information to be projected into a sonic image. This is precisely *because* musicians, thanks to notation, don't need to totally comprehend compositional messages in order for them to sound. Transhuman scale can be broached in music by redistributing individual creativity *out* of performance. Grandeur levies just a few costs.

Notation, in return, has to calibrate itself to the cognitive limits of an average interpreter. Specifications have to be trimmed to what can be relatively quickly assimilated by musicians who are already busily absorbed with their instruments and ensemble coordination. The more eccentric and complicated written directives, the more time and attention has to be dedicated to processing that information at the expense of these other concerns.

Notation connects most seamlessly when its language cleaves to the average, conventional and habitual. What can be easily graphed, and easily averaged, best adapts to being notated. Following the example of European practice, it seems as if pitch has shown itself to be the most adaptable sonic parameter for notation. It might even be asked how much of Europe's long time emphasis on melodic and harmonic development has been symbiotic with its system of notation.

Other sonic components — timbre — complex, compelling but indescribable sonorities and textures — rhythm — tend to have to creep in through the kitchen door — usually with the help of a composer who's willing to slip that door open while doing the uncharted heavy lifting and translation (Varèse, Ellington or Xenakis, for example). Conventional notation of rhythm — in contrast with its actual complexity — is schematically crude at best. And once again, it could be asked if the relatively primitive cultivation of rhythm in traditional Euroclassical practice has been in part due to how difficult the essentials of rhythm — beyond the baseline of durations — are to notate.

It's worth considering how the default biases of notation might precondition what's sonically cultivated. Being able to graph the relative durations of sounds introduces a fantastic investigative tool; but superimposing the stopwatch click track of technical time across music also opens a share of questions.

A graphic narrative illustrates "time" traveling in a straight line from beginning (represented as "left") to end (right). Time "really" does that? *Really?* The image portrays an undoubtedly useful tactical metaphor; but is it at all what either listeners or musicians *actually* experience as "time" — or rhythm — in (or out of) a musical context?

What about the commonplace presupposition in some musical circles that a beat (or pulse) is the inert — or "dumb" — stuff that measures out the "real stuff" of "music" that's doing the actual "speaking" — such as pitch, melody and harmony. It's true that rhythm portrayed as repetitive quantity can make for some pretty uninteresting viewing on a score; but the complicated vectors deployed during a Nuyorican montuno episode, for example, are anything but simplistic, mechanical repetitions. The multidirectional relationships among voices continually shift and redefine themselves in a way that never really settles or becomes "the same." And this is no accident at all because it's a deliberate accomplishment of design.

There's yet to be a rhythm theory formulated and articulated with the thoroughness and conciseness that's already been dedicated to diatonic harmony (although David Pleasant, Malcolm Braff and Leonard B. Meyer are among those who've been reaching in that direction). Theoretical rhythmic knowledge circulates in the face to face, person to person, experience based vernacular and is continually being rediscovered and worked out by each individual practitioner over and over; and it's thriving pretty well outside the corral of notation. The examples of both Indian and pan-African practice suggest that more rhythmic information can be efficiently encoded and transmitted via "nonsense" syllable complexes than can be easily encapsulated through visual representations. This can also be noted, for example, in how swinging so effectively eludes notated description.

The constraints on what can be intelligibly and smoothly grasped within any system of notation inevitably favor presets that encourage sonic presuppositions that, by default, eliminate, if not disadvantage, all of the sounds *not* represented within the system.

For example, the lattice of equidistant, tempered chromatic intervals, superimposed over the entire spectrum glissando of pitch, leaves out all the other pitches. Sounds too idiosyncratic, or too complex, to fit into conventional notation's apportioned slots may become habitually referred to as "noise." A descriptive tool such as notation can hardly avoid drawing insider-outsider oppositions that don't actually apply to the sound palette of the real world.

The immense conveniences of notation have to be accepted with at least some degree of salt. In relation to the genuinely laborious and complicated social cooperations that construct musical sound, notation often contributes a helpful shortcut. Shortcuts rarely tend to come cost free. The totally literate composer Charles Mingus preferred instead to convey the details of his sonic constructs by ear whenever possible because the entire process of assimilation, so amply informed by unnotatable details, differs so much from sight reading and yields a distinctively different musical motion, attitude and sound. Thelonious Monk would often only show a musician the sheet music for a composition after a musician had worked most of it out without the paper.

Music (and musical ideas) is expensive. It demands a lot of time and attention of its participants. Notation slam-bam cuts to "the point" and emphasizes the literal sound and result — which does minimize a lot of time consuming digestion and comprehension (and many, many times, composers are more than happy to have the option). It becomes possible to organize fly-by-night sonic realizations almost right on the spot (if the sight readers are competent). Beyond that, recordings and electronic sound generation can exponentially trump notation's ability with an amplified capacity to bypass the slow human challenges of information transfer in music. Well, sometimes there just isn't time to take the time. Really.

12

Metacomposition

A sonic community coheres around commonly recognized notions of sonic and gestural convergence. What might be called music's "protocompositional" footings share interactive dynamics with nearly any reciprocal social exchange. And generally, people have to mutually acknowledge some area of commonality in order to interact at all.

In playing music "together," some sort of connective thread, some way of "reading" each other's actions, some kind of referential context has to be developed in order for each participant's moves to make sense — not only to each other, but for oneself in relationship with that context as well. However provisionally, a system of mutual expectations about each other's sonic behavior becomes established. In a duo context, for example. the relationship formed by consensus and mutual regard would constitute a third member of the band — and all three would be gauging their adjustments toward whatever the sonic image happens to be doing.

Two very, very green, rookie guitarists who are trying to play together for the first time either already share musical ideals that they hope to emulate and realize — or if they don't, they're soon enough going to have to arrive at some kind of working agreement about what it is they're doing together — that is, if they're to continue playing Foundational social accord precedes the exact particulars of whatever sonic image emerges out of musical collaboration.

A compositional design manages to find itself sounded through alliance with a specific social milieu. This happens because actual performers are always going to have to fill in whatever gaps manage to perforate whatever body of compositional indications. No matter how well described, mapped, illustrated, demonstrated or explained such messages may be, performers have to bring yet something else that's not (or can't be) indicated by the compositional information being circulated. They add whatever they have to in order for the music to palpably *sound*. And, because the ways a gap can be filled is so susceptible to variation, the interpretive community a composer collaborates with makes an important difference in terms of the music's resulting sound. A composer has to be able to account *for* — and count *on* — the way one's collaborators process musical information.

The shared understandings around which these social cooperations gather aren't at all so incidental to a music's composition. Both the working assumptions and social interactions are influential constituents of a music's construction. A coordinator of sounds (which is what's ordinarily meant by the word "composer") has to therefore consider and incorporate a specific *community of practice* into the music as an inseparable component of its sonic design. In coordinating a sonic event, a composer collaborates with a range of customs and conventions that shape what might be called a music's *metacompositional* structure.

Metacompositions are socially shared pools of musical behaviors, assumptions, practices, techniques, experiences, methodologies and expectations that have been evolved through trial, error, experiment and circumstance by a multitude of musical participants over time. They function as compositional commons, as templates that are both everybody's and nobody's. They're "what everybody knows" (or is supposed to know) while contributing to a sonic event.

Metacompositions encompass all the compositional decisions that are accepted in advance as a context within which the *act* of composing (which is the choosing among sounds) can situate itself. In other words, most of any musical "composition" has *already* been composed collectively by a sonic community's coordinating conventions before a specific composer has even begun.

An individual composer may be able to noticeably tweak, influence, deconstruct, expand and, to some extent, transform elements of a metacomposition: but a metacomposition's more or less autonomic footings network a complexity that's way too dense for any individual composer to completely reinvent (or bother with reinventing) from scratch anyway. A composer's sonic influence in ensemble music is conditional and subject to conventional practices already in circulation

In a *very, very* rough analogy with verbal language, metacompositions articulate core *conventions* of a sonic community — as equally in the root senses of *convenience and gathering* as in the sense of common practice and assumption. Where the structure of a commonly spoken language can't help but influence the structure of interactants' exchanges; a composer can't avoid absorbing metacompositional decisions into one's own composing.

One could think of "metacomposition" as a relatively vast musical composition that's able to host very particular compositions or compositional acts. As a collectively formulated artistic "work," it already poses an aesthetic statement before any particular composer even begins to associate with it. A composer's choice of metacompositional context likewise voices aesthetic statement and compositional decision; and the individual responsibility a composer assumes for a metacomposition becomes *as if* one *had* composed it oneself. Such are the paradoxical wages of participation in communal creativity.

13

Metacomposition in Eurological Practice & 4'33"

A monological composer working in a conventional Euroclassical context accepts as a matter of course a wide swath of assumptions as built in components of the specific "composition" (sonic design) being constructed. The concert hall convention is assumed, within which an audience quietly attends to sounds emitted by an ensemble of literate performing musicians who act as representative agents of the (usually absent) composer's designs and intentions. Prevailing standards of intonation and instrument design, along with what kind of timbre and articulation can be expected from each performer are taken for granted as well. With so much structure *already* in place, it really is practical for a remote composer to commit a design to notation — and for that design to be sounded in pretty close correspondence with what the composer had in mind.

The remarkable resilience and strength of this elaborate and very particular metacompositional structure (an immense collaboration sustained by the collective efforts of many, many thousands of people over centuries) was remarkably demonstrated by the North American composer John Cage in 1952 with his composition *4'33"*.

Cage very cleverly leveraged Euroclassical concert hall conventions in order to *intentionally* frame a sonic portrait of "non-intention."

Listeners responded to notices announcing a concert to be presented by the Woodstock Artist's Association at Maverick Concert Hall in Woodstock, New York at 8:15pm on Friday, August 29. During the performance, listeners were seated before a performance area where pianist David Tudor sat at a piano, and placed a score on the piano and sat quietly. He alternately lifted and lowered the keyboard lid to indicate respective movements of the piece while timing the length of each movement with a stopwatch and turning pages at the appropriate moment. Listeners were able to hear the incidental sound of wind among the trees outside, a few raindrops on the roof, page turns and eventually, increasing human whispering and grumbling among the concertgoers.

Cage's construct was radically iconoclastic in terms of its sonic "content" in a way that's since exerted a powerfully enduring influence on the imagination of composers and listeners. Cage could argue rhetorically on behalf of "sounds in themselves:" but in order to introduce them as "music," he (ironically) reaffirmed the underlying metacompositional assumptions of Eurological concert music. The interaction structures segmenting the roles of composer, performer and audience remained intact and unchallenged. As Cage himself once put it, "Composing's one thing, performing's another, listening's a third. What can they have to do with one another?" Cage made sure that everything remained hands-off, non-interactive and non-reciprocal.

14

The Jam Session's Metacomposed Interactions

Metacomposing the Jam Session

The jam session is a profound social and aesthetic achievement. It could seem astonishing to a witness sufficiently unfamiliar with this sonic community, that *any* gathering of musicians (who themselves may never have met) would be able to instantly arrive at hours of richly coherent and inventive music with neither rehearsal, sheet music nor pre-recorded (or digitally pre-programmed) resources. The metacompositional frameworks that enable this apparently immediate fluidity have been developed, tested and altered by innumerable musicians as part of a long term, ongoing, community project.

Developed in Africanized North America, the metacomposition that informs a jam session constructs an immensely adaptable platform for dialogical composing. But as event, the jam session is also much more than just this. It consolidates an occasion for modeling and developing character while transmitting and transforming values and attitudes. All at once, it functions as school, workshop, symposium, experimental laboratory, sketchbook, proving ground, sparring gym, networking opportunity, celebration and dream pool.

In contrast with the exacting standardization of individual musicianship that's so pivotal to most monological organization, compositional and interpersonal heterogeneity is assumed in a jam session from the start. Contributors don't have to all be "the same" in this way — and it's actually a lot better if they aren't. The metacomposition coheres out of a more unevenly distributed common engagement in a pool of compositional knowledge and practices, of commonalities that are actualized more out of patchworked family resemblances than from any strict adherence to norms.

Any decentralized social organization necessarily depends on participants' self cultivation of autonomy and self reliance. Accordingly, jam session participants have to seize responsibility for their own musical knowledge, preparation and compositional initiative. An ability to hold one's own contributes to a common consideration for the whole, whether that be toward the symptoms audible through the global sonic image or via the collaborative relationships being forged through close, reciprocal listening and instant adjustments to each other's peculiarities, foibles and proclivities. This cooperative structure maintains the capacity to foster each individual's potentially going beyond the ordinary into something personally unique, not only through an aesthetic of open, mutual support, but through an intra-ensemble creative *competition* that expands the thresholds of creative musicianship and conception throughout a sonic community.

Successful participants aspire to model performance ideals already learned through previous listening, observing, conversation and direct trial-and-error experience. And, in tandem with the wide inventive freedoms nurtured by this structure, the accompanying dispersive entropy of free-for-all can be mitigated through a range of compositional devices that regulate and direct sonic behavior, most explicitly where a mismatch of a participant's preparation, skill, maturity or attitude with a situation disrupts or impedes access for other musicians to musical interactions at optimum intensities.

Epithets such as "You ain't playin shit" or "No playin motherfucker" have often been applied with great effect in acute situations where more underplayed messages seem to have been passing unheard. Pendergast era Kansas City lore recounts Jo Jones having conveyed an airborne cymbal toward the vicinity of a very young Charles Christopher Parker Jr. during one of his earlier jam session forays. Pruning a session's population may also be achieved somewhat less directly by adopting brutally fast tempos, very obscure tunes or especially unusual keys (skills for which the Yardbird himself later became notorious).

A player might step right across the path of another about to play. The session's leader may suddenly reprise the theme and take the tune out. The drummer or the bassist (or both) might suddenly go to the bar for a drink. A set may end unexpectedly without explanation. A player may be politely requested to sit out and listen. Or, one could be blankly stared *through* as if no human body could possibly be occupying the space that unfolds before the viewer.

Some of these techniques might provoke an impression of hostility (well, sometimes people really *are* hostile); but these devices could also be understood as instructive — as well as protective — regarding the creative spirit of the session (and besides, hostility or displaced ego seem to insert themselves as unremarkable denizens of just about any humanscape). The role of a musician who responds to these resistances with adequate agility, or who perseveres long enough to return someday in more able form, transforms from potential interloper to contributor. This is to say nothing of what's learned about oneself (and about the generating attitudes and structures of the music) through such experiences.

Depending on the situation, the tone of mutual support in a jam session can switch from challenge to nurture (which includes various blends along this spectrum). More experienced musicians may ease up on the intensity of their own invention in order to bolster the confidence of a developing musician. Common reference points, such as chords, the first beat of a chorus cycle, the "one" or the pulse itself may be stated much more obviously than usual to this end. The guiding ethic is not to exclusively exert one's own way, but to achieve successful music *as a group*, whatever it takes.

Links & Foundations

The most simple version of jam session metacomposition to discuss would be the most commonplace and clearly defined one; and that would easily be the old school, "classic" — what's now called *straight ahead* — species of jam session. This format encapsulates a common *lingua franca* that could conceivably allow generationally disparate musicians such as Mary Lou Williams and John Gilmore — or Anthony Braxton — to perform side by side without any one distracting from the strengths of the others.

Successful contributors to this particular species of jam session participate in specific metacompositional assumptions about the musical proceedings and organization that facilitate their composing together. These assumptions address the roles and behavior of different instruments, constructive principles and a common repertoire of interface structures.

The propensities of differing instrument families ground certain basic expectations around sonic comportment and behavior during this variety of jam session. The sounds of touch instruments (percussion, piano, plucked strings) generally decay fairly quickly after more abrupt and prominent attacks. The enfolding silences emphasized by these envelopes imbue a sonic transparency that allows these instruments to sound concurrently without any one obscuring the other. This, along with a relative ease in playing these instruments continuously, draws the tactile with the kinetic in forming the music's rhythm section.

The more continuously sustained sounds of breath instruments (and bowed strings) superimpose more opaquely. The need to inhale and to give one's lips a break yield more discontinuous blocks of sound; and the intervening silences accent the ongoing assertions of the rhythm section. These sonic and technical features generally displace wind and bow sounds away from rhythm section activity; and in the interest of sonic and narrative clarity (along with creative elbow room), improvised contributions from these instruments are customarily deployed sequentially, one at a time, as soloists.

Aligning instrumental roles around wind and touch generation parallels other important stereo articulations such as paired speech and gesture, storytelling with mime, or song and dance. But what might ably facilitate ensemble organization applies differently to the possible ranges of individual contribution. Each participant can draw from the entire spectrum of these modalities. Each may adopt solo, accompaniment or rhythm section articulation as needed, desired or preferred. Optimally, wind players must speak Percussion fluently, as touch instruments are clearly able to narrate as fluently in soloistic terms, while drums themselves sing, talk, tell, lead.

Common reference to an interface structure, such as a "tune" (12 bar blues, *I-Got-Rhythms*, Tin Pan Alley songs, or well known musician generated material) marks parameters for the application of instrumental roles. Percussion instruments, who deal in many untempered, "inexact" sonorities, emphasize the shapes and momenta of these patterns in their articulations and proportionings of time, rhythm, timbre, pitch and density. Instruments congenial to sounding multiple, tempered pitches simultaneously — such as those built with finger or mallet keyboards, or guitars — assume responsibility for sounding chord sequences within the group. The bass dwells between, emphatically a tuned drum with the pulse world while melodically grounding harmonic sequences for the tempered pitch world. Those players acting in a solo role assume responsibility for sounding melodic themes (the "head") as well as constructing their individual narratives as soloists.

Constructive principles gather around a generally predictable pulse that fulcrums compositional convergence and divergence, along with a distinct quality of rhythmic attentiveness and interaction that's recognized as *swinging*. Superimposed across this pulse community is a melodic theme (the "tune") in conjunction with a supporting harmonic sequence that describes a specific number of beats. This reference pattern (one cycle of which is known as a *chorus*) is continually reiterated, around which the ensemble organizes itself and individual solos are generated and measured. It's generally expected that players make aspects of these components audible in their inventions as a way of bolstering and reassuring ensemble focus and coherence.

This principle is complemented by a common understanding that each musician's contribution should make other individuals (as well as the band as a whole) "sound good," which is often achieved through including (however obliquely) some aspect of what each of the others are doing, as much through mirroring as by strategic omissions (silences) and divergences — both of which accent features that are already being sounded.

Extended variations on the generative principle of call-and-response further broaden this collaborative syntax. The custom of trading bars, where soloists alternate in groupings of 12, 8, 4, 2 (or even 1) measures demonstrates one very graphic example. Call-and-response is also deployed more subtly, as where one musician "completes" or punctuates another's phrase. Back and forth interchanges also become so densely rapid that, for all practical purposes, they turn simultaneous and mutually intertwined.

Signaling (even signifying) among musicians also encompasses a larger, common sonic world beyond the immediate circumstance. Patterns in common with predecessors, ancestors, coevals and competitors — either as acknowledgement, play or parody — enrich the music's composition with allusion. And a common convention such as the riff, for example, avails itself as a familiar component in constructing "instant arrangements" that urge soloists and cast relief to their individual improvisations.

None of these elements by themselves would seem to figure that importantly in musical construction; but taken all together, they describe a set of conditions for a metacompositional *community* that can then compose together dialogically. These common considerations foreground a degree of trust and confidence that allows each individual to stretch creatively without excessive and cumbersome concerns for the coherence of the entire musical organism. Working agreements are achieved around not only sonic parameters, but also regarding important modes of interaction that are clearly enough delineated that they needn't unduly restrict specific action.

Adorno's Jam Session Expertise

One prescient, if inadvertent, insight into the audible presence of metacompositional coordinates in a lot of dialogical music can be credited to the German philosopher, Theodor Adorno. While not having earned all that much regard among vernacular musicians, Adorno remains an important seminal thinker for the scholarly field now known as cultural studies. He was an ardent lover of music and wrote about it extensively, studying composition with Alban Berg and becoming a vocal champion of Arnold Schoenberg's music and the Second Viennese School. However, when unsympathetic, his writing can occasionally display an inclination toward zero-sum, winner-take-all polemics.

While the eminent cultural theorist reserved a lot more invective for the composer Igor Stravinsky, Adorno did publish, beginning in 1936, a number of derisive essays regarding what he understood to be "jazz;" although it's not really so clear exactly what he meant by this word. He may have initially been responding to Weimar era knockoffs of Paul Whiteman in Europe or might have meant any kind of commercially disseminated, "popular" music. Yet, in the 1950s, he manages to mention the word *bebop* as just another example of more-of-the-same; and even though he enjoyed a comfortable position at Columbia University during the early 40s, there's apparently no indication that he ever took a quick (less than 10 minute) cab ride over to Minton's or Monroe's to talk with, or listen to, Kenny Clarke, or Monk, or Charlie Parker.

Adorno seems to have assessed what he thought of as "jazz" as a sort of degenerate offshoot of notated European monological practice (it might have slipped off his radar that U.S. African musicians could actually have been appropriating European generated musical materials in the service of very, very different aesthetic applications). He could thus absolve himself to freely interpret this "jazz" as no more than a species of "mannerist interpretation," as "music which fuses the most rudimentary melodic, harmonic, metric and formal structure with the ostensibly disruptive principle of syncopation, yet without ever really disturbing the crude unity of the basic rhythm, the identically sustained meter, the quarter-note." He thus summarily dismissed this sonic community's "paltry stock of procedures and characteristics."

From a musician's perspective, it's unbelievably tempting to speculate as to how such an otherwise astute thinker could turn, in this instance, so slipshod concerning just what it is he actually means by "jazz," a term that would ordinarily connote the work of artists such as Duke Ellington, Charles Mingus, Max Roach or many members of the AACM (all of whom have, by the way, expressed, at the very least, a deep ambivalence concerning this "jazz" word themselves). But, assuming this is what the philosopher means, it seems odd that such a scholar of Marx would account so poorly for important variations in music's "conditions of production."

Adorno's admirable concerns about a general dumbing down of listening (with a corresponding circumscription of critical consciousness) might persuade more convincingly if he were describing instead some overly stylized, tightly formatted, commercially dictated *monological* music. However, the specific music Adorno targets is a dialogical one; and dialogical *listening* encompasses, and has to address, significantly different compositional circumstances than does attention to monologically organized sound.

A great deal of compositional activity, and hence compositional *meaning* in a dialogical context emerges through the relations *among* distinct compositional actors. While each contributor's inventions may separately achieve a degree of monological integrity, all of this is conditioned by, in relation with, and in reaction to, everything else developing *within* the ensemble. The global composition that a listener witnesses derives from the decisions of each contributing composer *and* their composite interrelations.

Because of this interactive complexity (a variety of complexity that's almost totally absent from monological constructs), novel and intricate musical messaging can evolve out of communications involving rudimentary, even mundane reference materials — and the transformations of these points of departure can be both subtle and profound. Yet, different as the elements and context are, from the point of view of each participant, dialogically composing from basic elements isn't operationally all that different from monologically developing an elaborate fugue out of a simple series of 4 pitches.

Social Philosophy of Polyrhythm

In terms of relational dynamics among participants, collective improvisation (dialogical composition) can be understood as a theatrical personification of polyrhythm. *Polyrhythm* emerges through juxtaposing and linking contrasting rhythmic patterns. Unlike syncopation, which describes a *single* pattern's displacement of a dominant pattern's accents, individual components of a polyrhythm sound with *equal* emphasis and importance. Conflict and difference among them throw into relief the individual distinctiveness of each contributing element. Yet at the same time, their differences together configure a harmonic relationship that can't be reduced either to their individual constituents or to any sum of these parts.

John Miller Chernoff's eloquent discussion of interrelating African ethics and aesthetics in his book, *African Rhythm and African Sensibility*, develops insights into African musical processes that parallel very strongly not just jam session interactions, but much (if not all) dialogically structured composition. His observations are so substantive that a good stretch of excerpts is quoted here.

> At an African musical event, we are concerned with sound and movement, space and time, the deepest modalities of perception. Foremost is the dynamic tension of the multiple rhythms and the cohesive power of their relationship. Founded on a sense of time and presence, the art of improvisation involves the subtle perfection of this rhythmic form through precision of perfor-

mance, complexity of organization and control of gestural timing. The act of creation is above all purposeful, never random, and the goal is balance and a fulfilling interdependence. As they display style and involvement, people make their music socially effective, transforming the dynamic power of the rhythms into a focus for character and community. We are even quite close to a metaphysics of rhythm if we remember that sensing the whole in a system of multiple rhythms depends on comprehending, or "hearing," as Africans say, the beat that is never sounded. ...

African affinity for polymetric musical forms indicates that, in the most fundamental sense, the African sensibility is profoundly pluralistic. One of the most patronizing Western biases regarding people in societies we call "traditional" is the notion that the events of their lives are nestled in and determined by the ready-made patterns of a culture they uncritically accept.

To maintain that poise in their social encounters, Africans bring the same flexibility which characterizes their participation in musical contexts: they expect dialogue, they anticipate movement, and most significantly, they stay very much open to influence. The many ways one can change a rhythm by cutting it with different rhythms is parallel to many ways one can approach or interpret a situation or a conversation. And there is always an in-between, always a place to add another beat. A musical occasion, like any other social occasion is therefore beyond any one perspective a person can bring to it, and people in Africa are usually realistic enough not to try to impose a single point of view on the larger context in which they are playing a part.

...The power and dynamic potential of the music is in the silence, the gaps between the notes, and it is into this openness that a creative participant will place his contribution, trying even to open up the music further. ... It is not only that one rhythm cannot monopolize all the notes; one rhythm means nothing without another. In a musical context, separation of parts heightens rhythmic

> dialogue, and in a musical ensemble, singlemindedness of purpose would be equivalent to poverty of expression.
>
> In a musical context, the diverse rhythms help people distinguish themselves from each other while they remain profoundly involved. ... From an African perspective, once you have brought a structure to bear on your involvements, and made your peace with it, the distinctive gestures and deviant idiosyncrasies of personality can stand out with clarity.

A continuity of African aesthetic values, as described here by Chernoff, with interactive ethics realized in a U.S. African evolution of the jam session shouldn't really be very surprising anyway. And some of what so ably informs jam session participation has been, and continues to be, influential and active well beyond the peripheries of any particular bandstand. Commonalities might be recognized in the ring shout, in freestyle exchanges among rappers, on basketball courts, in rapports between dancers or between minister and congregation in the Black church, in conversations — all this as well as in dialogues between master drummer and dancer in West Africa or between guimbri/sintir and trancer among the Moroccan Gnawa.

What's far *more* striking, however, is how remarkably *different* the jam session can be in accommodating what Robert Farris Thompson has adeptly identified as "apart playing." African polymetric organization is very clearly and carefully calibrated, and the exact details of each configuration are usually local to a very particular language community, region or even village. In contrast, jam session conventions evolved very quickly among a much larger and far more diverse population that's been in rapid movement across an entire continent. Adaptation to these circumstances had to yield a far wider, and even more pliable, span of variables for establishing this reciprocally defining "apartness."

The cultivation of a uniquely identifiable, instantly recognizable at first earshot, *sonic persona* (whether that be Bern Nix, Lester Young or so many others) has been held in high esteem for good reason. It's from the vantage and "way" of the distinct compositional actor (therefore both *personified* and, in terms of compositional choice, both interactively and dramatically *theatrical*), the unique sounds and telltale patterns of imagination, the characteristic (or unexpectedly *un*characteristic) compositional decision streams in interaction with all of the others (while, in Chernoff's words, "sensing the whole in a system of multiple trajectories") that establishes the diversity and tensions that "help people distinguish themselves from each other while remaining profoundly involved."

Some instances of dialogically generated music might not even *sound* "African" at all or, when extended, even explicitly "African American." Yet, the focus of listening, the attitudes toward collective composition, the animating intelligence and activities, of which the sound is a symptom, will still reveal deep kinship with what Chernoff describes regarding African attitudes and practices.

Repetition, Connection, Continuity

African or Indigenous American relationships with pulse as nuanced message seem to be absented from Adorno's more abstracted, notation framed notion of beats as no more than quantitative, mindless (if not mechanical) measurement devices. His critical framework excludes them as components of a music's "formal language."

For Adorno, internal repetition within a musical event (versus the verbatim, wholesale repetition of a fixed, monological work) breeds a predictability leading to a stereotyped banality that, in true domino theory sequence, retards not only listening, but *any* ability to independently draw distinctions about the world one lives in.

However, founding an indictment of a music upon its predictability maneuvers a pretty slippery slope. First of all, prediction (whether accurate or not) is a consistent companion of attending to *any* event, music included. Concurrently, each event settles toward a distinct *frequency* of predictability. A musical event that aspires to total discontinuity encourages an expectation that it will *continue* to behave that way, thus *predictably* so.

A more realistic notion of predictability would instead assess the dynamic tension invited *between* apparent predictability and divergent surprise as two interdependent components. Furthermore, Adorno seems to assume that predictability *really* is predictable, that the dangers of error, lapses in attention, dissolution or deliberate shifts in musical activity during performance are safely distant probabilities. Had he *ever* been on a bandstand?

Repetition without consideration may well doze off into some species of "banality." But, deeply considered repetition in tandem with carefully applied divergence reveals many of the fine distinctions to be discovered among apparently "predictable" beats (if one's listening with sensitivity and intelligence) that enrich and complicate, rather than enervate, a musical message. Chernoff, in noting that "a drummer uses repetition to reveal the *depth* of the musical structure," footnotes his observation by citing the Danish philosopher Søren Kierkegaard: "He who wills repetition is matured in seriousness."

Jacqueline Pettiford, wife of bassist Oscar Pettiford, reminded Downbeat Magazine in 2009 that as

> The son of a full-blooded Native American mother and half-blooded Native American father, Pettiford was exposed at an early age to Indian ceremonial music and dance, and he contended that the importance of the American Indian to jazz has been underestimated if not

completely overlooked. He maintained that the 4/4 tempo, which after all is the basic beat of jazz, came directly from the American Indian; that, though it existed in European music, it was not used in the same way.

Percussionist Newman Taylor Baker, once related that, in continuously playing a simple quarter note as ride (conceived as of swinging or "straight ahead" pulse), he simultaneously hears an unsounded, concurrent triplet quarter note pattern, actively hearing a beat that may be never sounded — a procedure solidly consonant with African practices. The impact of heard but unsounded musical components can't be discounted in terms of their influence on important microdetails of invention or on the direction of related inventions.

Metacomposition's "Paltry Stock"

But still, one does have to finally concede that Adorno really *is* right. A straight ahead jam session really *does* rely on "a paltry stock of procedures and characteristics." It's supposed to be *exactly* like that, and it's integrated this way intentionally and by deliberate design. Coordinating references such as "tunes," common pulses and chord progressions have to be *no more* than schematic so that they can adequately inform each participating composer's background awareness without ever overburdening attention necessary for the actual compositional choices at hand. This is a very practical accommodation of human cognitive capacities. If too rich, too detailed, too complicated, *too* unpredictable, metacompositional information would so distract an improviser that the composing process would simply seize and freeze up.

Saxophonist Marvin Blackman (*nee* Barbour), who worked extensively with Rashied Ali as well as with Art Blakey, has reaffirmed that these metacompositional supports are only additional coordinates superimposed over multipersonic, polyphonic and polyrhythmic activity that's *already* in motion. These less easily mappable attitudes, activities, procedures and interactions more substantively enact the music than these more mundane add-ons.

Adorno's complaint that "the schema shines through at every moment" manages to state what's often glibly obvious about coordinating dialogical music a lot of the time. Audible reference interfaces facilitate synchronization and communication among participating composers without leaning on notation (into which such supports can otherwise be offloaded and audibly disguised, if not hidden) or on conductors.

A "tune" in a jam session is neither "the music" nor is it the "composition" (both of which are discovered as performance). A "tune" functions much more like a *time line*, as a centripetal reference signal like the continual bell patterns sounded in much West African percussion music or the clave patterns that undergird so much Afro-Latin music.

In the jam session, even melodic cycles and harmonic progressions become appropriated as *rhythmic* coordinates (which was not at all the purpose for which they were originally developed during Europe's common practice era). The application of these components in Black music can often differ substantially from their customary functions in earlier European music.

Provincially Cosmopolitan

As for Mr. Adorno, his conception of how a music's formal language constructs a meaning seems to have limited itself to habitual monological concerns with *only* the notation friendly dimensions of a sonic artifact. Fixating on music's sonic design to the exclusion of its role within a composition's social structure reifies music by arbitrarily sundering the interdependent relations of musical sound and musical activity.

In listening to an aurally coordinated, dialogical music through literately circumscribed, monological ears, Adorno directed considerable philosophical acumen against a straw dog of his own creation, one very, very different from what its musicians have come to know through direct, practical experience.

And, if it weren't so genuinely painful, there might even be some ironic humor to find here. Adorno, himself a target of genocidal racism, concludes, with a summary judgement, that African American musicians were too stupid to notice that they were being oppressed and would therefore, unwittingly, and without the benefit of any critical thinking capacities, evolve their own music as a gesture of complicity with that status quo. Now, just what would Max Roach have said to that?

What's unfortunate is that, just as the credibility and affective power of D.W. Griffith's cinematic innovations ride forever tandem with his propaganda on behalf of white supremacy, Adorno's well earned prestige within the academy continues to lend credence (at least for a few well insulated, intellectual couch potatoes reclining behind ivory towers) to his far more erudite and genteel packaging of the same.

Mycelium to the Forest

That a jam session can, with its nearly self-depreciating, decentralized informality, be fun (and why shouldn't it be?) may mislead a casual witness about the actual profundity of its supporting meta-compositional structures, which have, over and over again, continued to prove themselves in practice as intricately sophisticated aesthetic resources. The jam session paradigm encapsulates a *way*, a mode of collectively generating music, that informs not only "non-idiomatic free improvisation" but the substrate assumptions upon which the great art of composing for improvisers (as so ably demonstrated by Ellington, Monk, Mingus, Ornette Coleman, Sun Ra, Cecil Taylor or Henry Threadgill) has been able to locate itself.

15

The Garden of Free Improvisation

Blank Boundaries

The jam session builds almost entirely on metacompositional frameworks to platform dialogical composing. But, probably the most dialogical of musical structures might be found amid contemporary free improvisation, where the jam session paradigm has been extended to incorporate sonic and interactive structures so unpremeditated that they can only evolve on the spot.

This extraordinarily receptive structure is capable of absorbing any sound, system of sound or way of sounding that has yet to discover a logic or systematization; and it reserves, potentially, a seat for everyone, from the cultivated musician to the adamantly non-musical to the purposefully idiosyncratic and the player of invented instruments or non-instruments. It can host a heterogeneity of sound generators, of sounds resistant to description or notation, of systems of musical thought, of vocabularies, of cultural experience, all together and simultaneously in whatever combination. Whatever couldn't happen anywhere else just might be possible within free improvisation. And, given the unlimited possibilities and generosity of this metacomposition, there are musicians who have significantly decided that, at least for them, free improvisation, *all by itself*, is enough.

The term "free" has been loosely applied to almost any nonstandard seeming improvisation that departs in some way from cycling metrical grids and/or common practice tonality, hence what's been called "free jazz" or the deliberately far more indeterminate "free music."

But, in its most exacting applications, free improvisation operates through a suspension of shared ensemble presuppositions as to what a music may become; and its sound and design are progressively developed *exclusively* from musician initiatives and responses as they occur in *situ*. This is often motivated through aspirations to discover yet unheard musics conceivably outside the prescriptions of style, genre or idiom.

Free improvisation, however, is not "free" in the sense of being totally unlimited. It's rather a highly specifying metacomposition whose constraints prioritize and sustain the compositional blank slate.

To work from a "blank slate" means to start from scratch, to find out what will happen and take it from there, valorizing in some ways what Allan Ginsburg frequently celebrated as "first thought best thought." How this differs most from the jam session is its elimination, or disavowal, of any commonly acknowledged compositional interface through which participants might communicate regarding the overall shape and direction of the music. No single contributor can access the music's sound and sonic image *as a whole,* which, among other things, parses scarce footing to those conceptual imaginations who incline toward ensemble or orchestral perspective.

Under the very best of circumstances, roles and relations among individuals are left open to discovery, but in the absence of such discovery, these interrelations have to be, at least within the "real time" of performance, glossed over or otherwise simulated, which is to say that the absolute liberty entrusted to each participating composer is, at the same time, enveloped within silences that limit, or even dismiss, collective provisions for a context responsive to individual input.

How Free is Free?

As structural method rather than sound, free improvisation is not bound to any particular signature sonority. No matter how attentively an individual may shape one's own sonic contribution, relations with the music's composite sound remains indefinitely slippery and ambiguous. The presumed "anything goes" permissions of free improvisation (especially within jam session varieties) have to therefore count for balance on compensatory listening, in other words, on self-editing, good manners, perhaps even protracted waiting. If so much as a single participant breaks decorum as egotist, exhibitionist or sonic bully, the entire interactive context is liable to implode.

Like any other structural system, free improvisation relaxes easily toward default tendencies and is no more insulated from habit driven stereotype than any other. For example, the high speed, high density, high decibel model of collective free improvisation demonstrated to a great extent on John Coltrane's 1965 recording of *Ascension* is still traffic jam emulated (well removed from its original context) over 50 years afterwards (this just happens to stretch about the same generational distance as between James Reese Europe and Coltrane, to put this in perspective,) as if something "avant-garde" is being realized versus yet another reaffirmation of an already long crystallized stylization.

And, paradoxically, explicitly non-idiomatic free improvisation may often have to define itself more through what it keeps at bay than by what it includes, not only in the eschewal of a common musical language, but in the deliberate exclusion of connective tissue and sonic gestures that might invoke any kind of idiomatic response, quite often averaging out, curiously enough, to soundscapes that most resemble Euroclassical constructions from the mid-20th century.

Absent the intermediate tensions of ensemble interface, some musicians might (or might not) be inclined most toward whatever is habitually most comfortable or convenient for them. More curious or inventive participants, particularly within free improvisation jam session contexts, might encounter a sensation of swimming upstream, of dodging black hole debris of cliché that potentially chokes any options beyond band-aid footnotes.

Pushed to its nadir, the liberties necessary to free improvisation can collapse into the entropy of laissez faire. Knowledge, awareness or skill can be cast as mere options rather than indispensable means to expansion of perception and imagination. Where the spectrum of possible compositional choices remains consistently "unlimited" (even if only in principle), one choice could be just as easily be as "good" as any other, and an overly congenial plurality of possible interpretations among participants might, rather than instigate combustion and discovery, neutralize the fertile tensions between imagination, sound and interaction.

Aspirations to stretch beyond the confinements of histories can devolve into perceived exemptions from histories that are still actively informing, nurturing, contrasting or impinging upon the current moment. The tensions and standards, such as varying notions of musicianship, that animate and clarify the meta-compositions, languages and dialects called idioms can come to be considered not only disposable, but not even worth contending with, learning from or being able to communicate with. What one's either incapable of hearing or doing might even be redefined as a desirable asset.

Often for very good reason, some well-seasoned free improvisers nevertheless most prefer the challenge of novel combinations of sound, circumstance and disposition met through ever varying assortments of collaborators; but such one-off settings, much like the jam session and one-night-stand pickup band, can also, conveniently enough, get by without laborious ensemble learning, preparation and rehearsal, and, at least for the moment, bypass both the social and aesthetic (not to mention economic) challenges of cultivating long term, slow developing ideas, sound and chemistry *as an ensemble.*

While nothing about this structure limits *individual* follow up, follow through, further evolution or preparation, the conditions of operating exclusively within a contingent and ephemeral "now," also restricts musical interconnection to the immediate, the circumstantial, to the catch-as-catch-can, and possibly all the way to the superficial.

When disparate sensibilities and vocabularies interact, couldn't more be developed beyond conjunctions at lowest common denominators? Could new terms or sounds go past pastiche and eclecticism, or collaged solipsisms, toward inclusive, perhaps unexpected syntheses? This might take time, deliberation, analysis, reconsideration, experiment, collective application, processes that don't exactly happen on the spot.

What about the sounds, textures, sonic images and varieties of coordinated thinking that absolute free improvisation necessarily forfeits? What about unisons or synchronized countercurrents, whether pitch, melody, time or rhythm?

Free: Not Easy

The intrinsic liabilities of pure, free improvisation, like any other system, can be, and are, exceeded by extraordinary individuals and/or exceptional situations. And, while, unlike other structural formats, free improvisation can accommodate a sort of faux primitivism, this is not at all how the convention evolved.

The practice grew instead out of questions pursued by some of the more sophisticated and probing among musicians. Lennie Tristano, Ornette Coleman and Joe Harriott, for example, recorded some of the earliest documented examples of spontaneous collective composition free of any repeating reference grid. They extended what had already been happening in King Oliver's Creole Jazz Band and so forth to every aspect of musical formation.

Their compatriots had already worked closely with one another and were familiar not only with the original material and compositional systems of the bandleaders but were likewise fluent in the metacompositions underlying blues, jazz and bebop languages. These commonalities magnetized a communicational "glue" that allowed their music to stretch margins without disconnection or incoherence.

Derek Bailey, who later became one of the most effusive proponents of blank slate free improvisation, described, in a chapter of his book *Improvisation,* the very gradual, two year process that he and his collaborators went through in discovering how to do it.

Steve Lacy recounted that his transition into the free evolved at a similar pace, and it likewise appears that John Coltrane's extension of his own vocabulary and concepts into the pandirectional evolved step by step.

For those who were among the first to assimilate free improvisation, the process was, for them, anything but trivial. This is understandable because, when aspiring to the standards of impact, clarity, and persuasiveness achieved through other musical means, free improvisation reveals itself as perhaps the most challenging of all musical arts.

Alternatively, free improvisation could be instead enjoyed as a sort of live sonic laboratory, where ongoing experimentation investigates no more than how sounds might behave in varying circumstances.

Free Association

There are some free improvisers who see what they do as being free of the tyranny of the composer and conceive of the practice as an essentially anti-compositional procedure. But free improvisation is not at all "free" of composition, given that the major defining condition of any dialogical music is that participants compose. Furthermore, the social agreement that is composition, often consciously and voluntarily, incorporates ensemble decisions that influence and direct the music that is discovered in performance.

Taking into account the uniqueness of each individual, one of the most influential of compositional decisions in any dialogical music is *who's* playing. Sometimes, even non-participants (such as programmers, curators, producers or promoters) play this role of composer when they coordinate free improvised "encounters" the way George Wein chose whom to put on stage in his Jazz at the Philharmonic concertized jam sessions.

Compositional design at the ensemble level, that is to say, a collectively identified and recognizable interface, emerges as a component of the free improvisation of groups who play together repeatedly. The shared experience of playing together itself, an evolving mutual recognition and trust, and acquired expectations regarding each other's likely musical behavior together crystallize in some way, even if unspoken, a compositional matrix unique to that collective. And, after a while, such a band may reveal a distinctive sound and *way* that casts an ongoing and evolving predictive compositional ambience across its improvisations.

Ensemble composition becomes even more explicit where collaborators also share reflection, critique, suggestion and redirection that exert a distinctive formative influence on the music. As this sense of collective composition becomes more deliberate, free improvisation, in its strictest meaning, becomes less "free," while the music's "blank slate" acquires more and more of marks of composition for improvisers.

Free improvisation is not pure. It didn't evolve, doesn't happen, and doesn't sustain itself in a vacuum. It would be pretty rare indeed to encounter a participant in free improvisation who's had no experience whatsoever in any other other mode of musicking. Free improvisation operates amid a pluralism of options and takes advantage of their differences to define oppositional positions while drawing upon *all* kinds of musics and skill sets as indispensable resources.

16

Mixed Strategies: Composing for Improvisers

Redefining the terms "composer" and "composition" challenges, plays with and complicates the customary usage of these words (conventions pretty unlikely to change much any time soon). The already entrenched notion of "composer" corresponds with the familiar monological model developed through a millennium or so of practice in traditional Europe.

However, improvisers are also composers who work within conditions shaped by reciprocal interaction with other compositional agents. These *collective* improvisers are more properly recognized as *dialogical composers.* Nevertheless, improvisers also collaborate with musicians whom they themselves call "composers." This role can be most usefully described as a *composer-for-improvisers* (or, in other words, as a composer *for* other composers).

A composer-for-improvisers appropriates many of the tools of the strictly monological composer but applies them dialogically. In conventional monological practice, performance accomplishes the terminal endpoint of a compositional process. However, a composition for improvisers, in contrast, intervenes more as crossroad than destination and functions to set into motion *further* compositional activity during performance. It presents and proposes to each contributor leveraged topographies of orientational resistance for compositional listening, networks of channels, dams, diversions, floodgates, deep pools and rapids to spark and irritate the way a sand grain might elicit the growth of a pearl.

The sonic image of this sort of dialogically oriented "composition" may (or may not) in many respects resemble a monological one. But, there's also a parallel function in play that's dealing double meanings absent from monological procedure. A composition for improvisers proposes not only a sonic design, but a specific interactive matrix that enables common areas of reference and departure. It consolidates and choreographs relationships, interactions and developments that would otherwise be forged ad hoc, or left to metacompositional convention, and challenges participating dialogical composers to discover their own individual relationships with the proposed interface and to act on it in their own ways.

Within commonplace jazz understandings, the term "composition" denotes whatever sonic and interactive specifications are adopted beyond the common baseline of a jam session. Some of what's been called "arranging" (as with Gil Evans' work, for example) may actually reconstruct sonic activity at deep compositional levels. The collaborative head arrangements of the early Count Basie Orchestra or the cooperative compositions of the Art Ensemble of Chicago collectively realize compositional matrices, but most of the time it's been individuals who've been generating these "compositions" for collective improvisation.

• • •

Thelonious Monk and Charlie Parker, by way of their contrasting strategies, illustrate the impact composition delivers in dialogical music. Parker channeled his primary attention through instantaneous saxophone statements. His extraordinarily dense melodic "heads" are almost all superimposed over commonplace jam session frameworks: blues, *I-Got-Rhythms* and standard show tunes. This allowed an immediate grafting of his radically new conceptions onto templates that were already being shared within his sonic community and made it possible for him to reopen his ongoing compositional continuum with any competent pickup band, almost at the drop of a hat.

A Monk composition, however, proposes much more than another, conceivably interchangeable, "tune". Each describes not only a very specific sonic landscape, but particular regions of musical thinking and inquiry, all of which are embedded in the composition's phrase patterns and pitch combinations. Each sound in a Monk construct announces a distinct identity that addresses itself directly to the attention of a musician assaying the matrix.

Every component, from walking bass to standard harmonic progressions and resolutions, emerge rethought, reconsidered, reinvented and enriched. To treat a Monk composition as one would a jam session vehicle is also to close one's ears for a more generic excursion. In a Monk composition, nothing can be so taken for granted, and this necessity is built right into the music's sound structures.

Monk's example distinguishes the "composition" in jazz and other dialogical music from the "tune." A "tune," while pliable to stylistic variation, doesn't *require* any serious departure from conventional assumptions and treatment. However, a "composition," in this sense of the word, redefines the terms of a musician's engagement and proposes structures, concepts and interactions alternative to mainstream habits, and creates, to some degree, its own micro-idiom, or idiolect, which has to be assimilated by each contributor.

Ornette Coleman, likewise, did much more than construct "tunes" and blow on them, but his redirection of common practice was even more thoroughgoing than Monk's. And, although his example is seminal to the later evolution of open and free improvisation, Coleman was as concerned with each contributing voice being *heard equally* as he was with the individual liberties accorded to each. Coleman's structural solutions imply that an actualization of egalitarian social aspirations, whether in musical structure or anywhere else, may need to be more than random.

By playing "the music and not its background," which is to say, composing without a repeating reference grid, Coleman created a situation that transformed the function of rhythm section instruments. Bassists and drummers became foreground players, melodic in (and on) their own terms, and just as responsible for the evolution of the music's sonic image (or "form") as anyone else in the group. Coleman eventually more or less codified a system of developmental relations among lines, rhythms and players that he called *harmolodics,* a formulation more fundamental to his composition for improvisers than any particular thematic material he may have adopted at any particular moment.

This system of listening and interrelating, of flexibly transposing interpretations, seems to energize a centrifugal/centripetal dynamic that allows for the independence, interdependence and mutually reciprocal definition through contrast (perhaps not so different in principle from pan-African polyrhythm) of participating voices. Coleman's own citing of parallels with Jackson Pollock and the geodesic structures of Buckminster Fuller seems totally apt. And, Pollock himself had, by the way, (as cineaste Arthur Jafa has insightfully assessed in an essay entitled *My Black Death*) assimilated Black rhythm and dance (perhaps even despite himself) into his own process via jazz.

Harmolodics, as a holistic relational framework that depends on a synergy of components, is difficult to dissect into easily bounded, discrete elements and seems famously difficult to describe. However, Coleman's compositional design can also be recognized through its practice and effects. His music consistently resonates a distinct sound. The interaction of voices within maintains an audible tension and clarity that's anything but lax. No participant absorbed these compositional concepts instantly, and that learning took some time. Ornette Coleman worked closely with very small circles of musicians over extended periods rather than operating through fly by night associations. None of this is accidental.

In contrast, some composition for improvisers redirects meta-compositional information as both Miles Davis and John Coltrane often did with their regular working groups, primarily by way of how they played, choice of personnel and attention to interactive chemistry, sometimes even without saying a word. This might not at all seem like "composition" from a monological perspective, and there may have been no paper score anywhere in sight, but both Coltrane and Davis aimed for and accomplished the ensemble sound they were after, even when they were employing standard tune reference matrices. Their ensemble composition was consistently effective and successful.

Duke Ellington is, more than most, associated with the art of scripting for personalities, for compositional personae as well as their instruments, for Johnny Hodges in particular rather than conceivably anybody's generic alto saxophone. (One circulating, unattested story is that Ellington didn't write for an individual until he'd seen how he played poker.) Ellington's sound and method was interdependent with his musicians. He might appropriate ideas or phrases from band members' improvisations and incorporate them into his sonic tapestries and, in this way, sustain a feedback loop where musicians' ideas transform the sonic environment within which they operate. However, Ellington treated his orchestra primarily as *his own* instrument, and it could be argued that much of his written composing was a decades long continuous improvisation, during which various material might be extended, reorganized and developed.

Charles Mingus exemplifies ensemble composition as a means to raise the level of each participant's conception and improvisation (and, by extension, an entire sonic community) beyond any preconceived capacity. Mingus played provocateur to his fellow musicians as composer — and as bassist — and as bandleader — in pushing the thresholds of what an interactive matrix could demand of its musicians.

John Stevens and Joe Giardullo are among those who've invented compositional systems for improvisers that predict no specific sounds whatsoever, but instead, through fairly schematic but nevertheless comprehensive indicators, propose where to pay attention, how to listen, how to interact, which turns out, with proper care, to be enough to accomplish a common matrix and social agreement in the generating of a composite sonic image.

• • •

Any composition, as a plan for action, proposes a dream to be enacted by a sonic community, however provisional that community might or might not be. In addressing both overall sound and interactive conditions, composing for improvisers navigates a hybrid position between the global perspective of monological procedure and free improvisation's slimmer horizons while diverging from the status quo defaults of metacomposition.

Composers-for-improvisers themselves tend to be improvisers who imagine beyond their particular instrumental role, hear the ensemble as an integrated whole and invent some way to act from that. It's not such a stretch to imagine that, not only could this expand, and expand on, a composer's own sonic "vision," but that it might set in motion a sonic and relational world within one might be able to act more as oneself, where one's own peculiar curiosities, proclivities and ideas might find an actual place, might grow, flourish, be heard, witnessed, experienced and take effect.

As much as it is experiment, a composition-for-improvisers formulates a declaration of common meeting points recognizable by all who are participating. These function as homeostatic thermostat, as a network of markers with signaling potentials for collaborative construction and intra-ensemble communication. It enables collective focus on the development of specific inquiries, explorations, sonorities, relationships and strategies that can be cultivated through multiple performances over an extended length of time. Discoveries during performance can be integrated into working presumptions and fed back toward still further extemporaneous invention.

Whatever the design, the intended effect is collective and directed toward fellow dialogical composers, whether this be to light up some of musicians' hidden best or to disrupt habit and cliché and impel improvisation somewhere beyond where it would ordinarily go.

The strength of a composition-for-improvisers can be estimated in its proportioning of information in relation to live invention (its intelligibility and opportune malleability) and in its resilience — its ability to both fire up invention and withstand the ongoing challenges, variations and divergences continually launched by improvisers without losing its identity, tiring or going stale.

17

The Conduction Synthesis

Another significant, and significantly different, means of channeling compositional information that's evolved has been called *Conduction*® by Lawrence D. "Butch" Morris. Conduction is a dialogical reappropriation of the role and position of the Eurological orchestra conductor of monological music. Through conductors, musical information flows the way electricity travels through copper or light travels via fiber optics.

Monological conductors add live gestural notation to the one-way-street specifications already embedded in paper-and-ink notation and is especially effective, even necessary, while coordinating units at the scale of a symphony orchestra. Conduction amplifies the reach of this function by facilitating back-and-forth, give-and-take volleys of compositional information — heat transferring from, or through, one body to another, as it does in thermodynamic conduction.

The practice of coordinating musical sound through hand movement, or *chironomy*, very likely extends back well into unverifiable prehistory and has been documented to have been in use at least as long as 3500 years ago. Both monological conducting and conduction participate in this long continuum of problem solving, experiment and practice. The challenge of how to redirect a musical event in progress in response to unexpected circumstances (as well as to stagnation) or to sudden ideas and discoveries is not exactly intractable, but it is complicated enough to generate a broad plurality of strategic responses. Some of those who've applied hand signals as live, compositional intervention during performance include Lucas Foss, Leonard Bernstein, Sun Ra, Frank Zappa, Doudou N'Diaye Rose, Earle Brown, Alan Silva, Charles Moffett, Walter Thompson (all of whom were acknowledged by Morris), Adam Rudolph, Karl Berger and a widely expanding number of others.

Morris' book *The Art of Conduction* summarizes his own practice and thinking while distinguishing his particular understanding and use of the process from those listed above. "I do not draw stylistic lines between the ensembles, communities or musicians I choose to work with or the music I make." Identifying transmission, communication and expression as "a common ground where all culture and style cohabit," Morris refined his lexicon of directives to accomplish what neither monological means nor improvisation are able to access, operating between "notation" (monological crystallizations of sonic design) and dialogical composition (improvisation) in such a way that even a large orchestra might engage the degree of spontaneity, ignition, combustion, and momentum intrinsic to an improvising trio.

A trio needs no traffic lights, but as the number of participants in an improvising ensemble increases, cross-communications complicate toward an opacity that begins to weigh individually restrictive. This is a paradoxical vulnerability of free improvisation that monological procedure avoids altogether by separating composer and performer. The hybrids of composed or metacomposed interactive matrices manage to balance clarity of design and freedom of movement and association, but conduction invents yet another response to this in externalizing a music's information flow and channeling that through indicative (or interrogative) gesture.

The from-the-outside-listening-in perspective that a dialogical conductor shares with a monological composer facilitates hearing an overall, evolving soundscape in ways that no participating player can from *inside* the music. But, unlike the monological composer, a dialogical conductor engages with a soundscape in flux whose destinations can't be charted. Positioned as ringside witness to interactive exchanges among participating instrumentalists, the conductor is able to gauge reactions and effects, deduce some of the emergent logics in progress, spontaneously initiate compositional decisions and, through the somatic notation of gesture, intervene to redirect and accentuate what's evolving amid the ensemble.

However, to conclude that, just because all eyes need to focus on these signs and signals, that a dialogical conductor is in some way acting as a commander in the monological sense would be to overlook the more multilayered complexities of this innovative musical role. From the vantage of the other performers, the conductor presents a mirror, a physical image of the music's impact on audience, as feedback. But, this conductor is also no less improviser, no less initiator, no less dialogical composer, no less *player*, than anyone else in the band, except that the instrument being played is a silent one.

In Morris' words:

> The Conduction Lexicon is descriptive rather than prescriptive; its function is not to set limits but to test boundaries. Directives are indeed interrogative in nature, in that they ask the instrumentalist: "What does this sound like in this situation at this time?"

That Conduction signals are visible rather than audible situates the conductor-as-composer totally dependent on the reflexes, awareness, imagination, trust, respect and care emanating from an ensemble. The uniqueness of this position means that conducted directives find their most effective impact in relation to the overall shape of what an ensemble develops.

However the conductor is also at the same time just another member of the band who happens to be playing what is, in this case, an instrument of signs. Provocation and subversion — antagonistic cooperation — shaking up the status quo, may figure no less importantly than they might for any other improviser.

Because conduction addresses information flow among interacting compositional streams more than specific determinations of sounds, metacomposition (idiomatically shared compositional assumptions) turns renegotiable. Conduction directives may revise, update and reorganize the relations and mutual expectations of participating dialogical composers as the music discovers its own soundshape.

As metacomposer, a conductionist invokes what Anthony Braxton would term *transidiomatic* conditions in, as Morris put it, "an investigation of a new social logic that can unite and enhance existing traditions." In some ways, the compositional structure of conduction parallels those kinds of intersectional decision processes where diverse stakeholders and perspectives attempt together to forge resilient, although as of yet unforeseen, links and bonds.

Within a brain, synaptic pattern, the variety of possible associations, conceptions and ideas, overwhelmingly outnumber the available neurons. Synapses happen *in-between*, which is exactly where Morris' imagination and questioning led in his explorations of conduction.

Conduction is especially in-between in that its focus is relational. It has a little bit of (is in touch with) everything, but no one thing in particular, all of which consolidates a historically new kind of compositional structure and *way* constituted of elements that had already been right in front of everyone's face. And, rather than posing a replacement alternative to other compositional structures, conduction is able to ally with any of them, expanding and enriching the range of compositional activity without having to deny or take anything away.

PART THREE:
Other Thoughts

18

The Electronic Trickster

Musician

Even though recording technology has been in circulation during a span that's still, even now, more brief than seven generations, there are likely very few alive who've never encountered recorded sound being presented as "music." The impact of this has waxed so ubiquitous that it's turned easy to forget, easier to take for granted, and possibly difficult even to imagine, that the preceding millennia before millennia of musical practice had never encountered, much less had to contend with, a detachable facsimile of its audible surface such as this.

Like photography, which recounts the impact of reflected light absent any other components of that instant within which a lens opens, recording apprehends the *sound* of a musical event, but not the *actions* that constitute the music. Decontextualizing sound this way separates it from the people who generate it, and, in that transaction, relieves it of what Walter Benjamin might have called in his essay *The Work of Art in the Age of Mechanical Reproduction*, a sound's musical *aura* — "its presence in time and space, its unique existence at the place it happens to be" — which, in musical terms, would mean, at the least, the conceptions, interrelations and transformations among those generating the sounds.

Recording one-ups the Euroclassical ideal of "music" as a sonic artifact in its capacity to deliver a sonic image so thoroughly desocialized that it's no longer beholden in any way to its musicians. If sound reverberates the flower of a music, what recording does is pluck that part off as it dispenses with the plant. It far outpaces monological performance in its preservation of, and fidelity to, a particular sound and sonic design while granting composers even greater remove and acuity of perspective than notation could ever provide. A "performance" of recorded sound dictates a unidirectional flow of information into auditory space. It delivers an imperturbably stable sonic object that's already foreclosed on compositional interaction.

This is to say that the compositional structure of recording — its conversion of live and/or studio generated sound into fixed, exactly repeatable sonic "material" — figures far closer to most classical pan-European musical practice than it does to any open-system, dialogical structure. Neither musician nor those sound designers ordinarily referred to as "composers" are who compose a recording. Who composes a recording is its producer. The producer (who may or may not also act as musician and/or composer) is the person who finally decides which sounds happen when.

• • •

The degree of a producer's compositional intervention can vary by situation and intent. In documentary recording, for example, producer decisions tend to defer toward musicians/composers/performers. This is an especially important role because recording doesn't listen. It comprehends no distinctions between whatever musicians may want listeners to notice and concurrent sound distortion, traffic noise, conversation, wind, slamming doors or static. To compensate for this, a documentary producer simulates the seeking, focusing, filtering and emphasizing that listening would ordinarily imbue upon a live sonic event through choice of microphone placement, room ambience, stereo pan, volume adjustment, equalization, mixing, mastering, and whatever other tools may be at one's disposal.

The homology of recorded sound with monological presentation could encourage an interpretive musician, as it did Glen Gould, to eschew live performance altogether. However, the entanglements of recording with dialogical music are far more paradoxically complicated. One might start with one of recording's most important achievements, which is its export of memory beyond the endurance of a living body. Before this, Niccolo Paganini, for example, may have left notation, but his unique individual sound has nonetheless vanished. Buddy Bolden's legendary sound has since become no more than a story.

Recording interposes a sort of "double consciousness" (and this is not to trivialize the destabilizing precarity that DuBois was addressing with this term) in its summoning of a sonic *doppelgänger* that allows a composing performer to hear one's own sound almost as if one were instead hearing it from the outside as audience, in that way evoking potentially the eerie disparity that might also be felt between one's intimately projected self image versus an "objective" photo or video presentation. What recording accumulates of live performance might be also be taken as reverse notation available for later contrast or confirmation of what one may have thought was happening at the time.

Louis Armstrong, the most easily identified inventor of the contemporary role of extemporizing soloist, is said to have carried a tape recorder with him and to have listened afterwards to each performance. Cecil Taylor, who had initially seasoned with his mother's friends in the Ellington Orchestra, once told his bassist Lisle Ellis that he hadn't been able to really understand why so many were upset by his playing until he heard his first album.

Previous to recording, dialogical musics could only rely on person to person transmission of values and knowledge — in other words, on tradition — to sustain metacompositional continuity and context. A master of Carnatic, Hindustani or many West African musics (to mention just a few) would ordinarily apprentice for a couple decades before becoming oneself a vehicle adequate for passing on a tradition's musical information with the integration and congruence of one's predecessors. Recording, however, dislocates, syncopates, disembodies (at least temporarily) and accelerates these transfers.

Without recording as coevolutionary accomplice, dialogical music would not have developed the way it has since the 1920s. Newly paralleled by this instant archeological repository, composing-from-the-inside-out became augmented with a shadow of stability that, previously, could only be sustained though either highly specifying traditional behaviors or monological organization. With sounds engraved into vinyled recurrence (or later through tape or digital code), it became no longer necessary to *personally* repeat in order to remember. One could move on to something new with perhaps less encumbrance but also with a firm new wall at one's back as challenge to *not* repeat oneself — or, at the least, to not thoughtlessly repeat oneself.

This reverse notation could not only document a coordination of sounds as if it *had* been scripted, it further enhanced these representations with verbatim evidence of tone, delivery, timbre, timing, etc., all of which would be otherwise too burdensome to write down, much less adhere to.

Such a reliably unfluctuating, and, at the same time, portable, medium revolutionized the distribution of musical ideas. Compositional information could, especially with radio's collaboration, travel and diffuse like news bulletins, far swifter than person to person contact, easily amenable to detailed, autopsic analyses and interpretation, and capable even of slipping around checkpoints such as class divides, Jim Crow, national boundaries and authoritarianism.

Sonic rumors could, by means of recording, run well in advance of the actual presence of Armstrong, or Ellington, or Bessie Smith, Charlie Christian or Parker, Ornette Coleman, Jimi Hendrix or Miles Davis; and it became possible for an aspiring player to learn a band's entire book, and conceivably be ready to handle that music on the bandstand, without ever having witnessed the music in person.

A symbiosis developed wherein musicians provided producers with sounds to record while recordings cataloged part of what had formerly disappeared with performance, thereby enriching the possible scope of musician reflection, comparison, study and preparation. But, musicians weren't taking these maps for the territory itself. Recordings weren't, as of yet, accepted as substitutes for the "real thing," nor as some kind of last word, but rather as tools, snapshots, shorthand footnotes, clues as to what might be possible to actually achieve in practice.

What recording furnishes to both listener and musician is not actual music, but an exceptionally serviceable caricature. And, as with that two dimensional slice called a photograph, perception depends on interpretive associations donated by a viewer or listener. A viewer would assemble a very different composite from an image of a close companion versus an image of someone with whom one's not yet acquainted. A music's performing musician would likely fill in a recording's sonic silhouettes in greater correspondence with the initial event than anyone else, while other participants within that same sonic community, (listeners included) would hear those sounds at a more clearly specified grain than would someone farther removed from the music's generative circumstances and even more unfamiliar with its languages & intents.

This enormous utility aside, experience nevertheless alerts musicians that live sound delivers far more complex and nuanced information than any recording can. The sound of an instrument, or a voice, or a band, coming out of a little box exerts a distinctly different corporality than if it were generated in person. Despite this, a recording's listeners often quickly adapt with some likely to be fast forgotten magical thinking that pushes aside such inconvenient distinctions.

...

Overly presuming upon the swift fragility of any recording's links with its living predecessors nevertheless continues to deliver consequences for practice. Live performance demands more than emulating a recording's appearance, and dialogical composition exceeds recitation.

What recording is not able to explicitly encode is *how* a particular body of sound is generated. It can't reconstruct the immediate contexts that inform the sounds with meanings. Plenty can be inferred, but these inferences still have to depend on whatever experiences one may or may not be bringing to that encounter.

The more a musician bases what one does on recordings versus personal experiences, the more the resulting sounds tend to resemble caricature. There's no question that this type of emulation can foundation a learning curve, but that curve has to, at some point, arc toward basing one's actions on one's own understandings versus speculative impressions of someone else's. This is because composing structurally divulges first, not third, person narrative; and if a listener craves quotation, recordings offer a far more honest and reliable source.

This often deceptive mute dismemberment so innate to recorded sound, what Canadian composer R. Murray Shaffer has called *schizophonia* (the gulf between a sound's initial emergence and its electronic replicant), leaves a lot to the imagination. A chasm opens to fantasy, wonderment, guesswork, free association, outright misinterpretation and misapprehension seeping between gaps in the crossroad. Even dehydrated sonic imagery such as this persists nevertheless as DNA for possible, perhaps yet to be imagined musics; and recorded sound can still, often enough, mysteriously transcend these physical impediments and impart life force well beyond the dubious promises and insufficiencies of simulation technology. While mutation might sidestep exact replication toward misfire and mishap, it can also spawn genetic diversity. Wherever one listener may be getting it "wrong," someone else might be finding a new idea.

Producer

In a 1979 New Music New York talk given at the Kitchen in Manhattan's SoHo called *The Studio as a Compositional Tool* (later published in Downbeat Magazine), producer Brian Eno astutely summarized the shifting topography and widened opportunities that recorded sound introduces into sound design. Importing the sensibilities of his own earlier visual art studio practices, he notes that recorded sound spatializes what had previously been experienced as temporal and ephemeral. Working with "frozen" sound in a sound studio:

> Puts the composer in the identical position of the painter — he's working directly with a material, working directly

> onto a substance, and he always retains the options to chop and change, to paint a bit out, add a piece, etc.

Eno's estimate follows not only the precedents of the Italian Futurist embrace of noise, but also musique concrète, as developed by Pierre Schaeffer and others in the 1940s and 50s, where sound recorded to magnetic tape could be manipulated and extended through splicing, rerecording, speed changes and superimposition to construct sound bodies totally inaccessible via musicians playing acoustic, or even electronic, instruments.

The sound studio as instrument enables sonic imagination at scales far broader than any available to composers for musicians and instruments. Sounds, any sounds, even humanly impossible sounds — as well as acoustically improbable sounds — may be coordinated in any combination. Conceivably free at last of such potentially misinterpretive intermediaries as metacomposition, notation, conductors or performers; compositional intuition, bolstered with the exceptional convenience of immediate playback, may be able to react and intervene more influentially than wherever filtered through the preconceptions of any musician's acquired techniques. The emergent option of repeated listening to a block of recorded sound, something impossible to avail through live practice, can become a key component of the studio compositional process, as Eno elaborates:

> You're in a position of being able to listen again and again to a performance, to become familiar with details you most certainly had missed the first time through, and to become very fond of details that weren't intended by the composer or the musicians. The effect of this on the composer is that he can think in terms of supplying material that would actually be too subtle for a first listening.

One is able then, within the limits of studio technology, to emphasize and manipulate recorded material into sound bodies that may barely resemble what originally registered to a microphone. A studio composer is positioned, like a notation enabled monological composer, outside of the actual sound generation and likewise gains overall, orchestral perspective, with more or less absolute lineal control, over an issued sound body.

But, as instrument, the studio also democratizes access to the means of production and avails this absolute control to anyone who can afford and manage the technology. One no longer need practice or collaborate as musician in order to generate musical sound. In principle, absolutely *anyone* can do this.

• • •

Once "complete," these studio generated sonic constructions withdraw from the active human world into a sort of cold storage, a suspended animation that paper composers have long bemoaned as the lonely oblivion of the "desk drawer," that limbo of unsounded, or never to be heard, sonic imaginings.

Later reactivation, which is to say, *playback*, enacts a nearly robotic parody of monological performance. Speakers project whatever a recording dictates. No performance, no enactment, not even understanding is necessary. No *body* be present. And, these aural documents themselves would be nothing if not for a prosthetically extended neuronal network that enlists equipment manufacturers, electric power grids, broadcasters, cobalt and coltan mines in Congo, marketeers, petroleum refineries and more.

And, just what would a recording be without listeners? The *Golden Record*, lodged within the Voyager space probe launched in 1972 toward places unknown (such a beautiful idea grounded in so marvelously quixotic assumptions) catalogued some choice human musical sound for a yet to be discovered audience. Who along the way might be endowed with both the appropriate auditory capacities and the right gear? Herman Blount may be one to answer that question. Meanwhile, back on Earth, an online discovery engine named Forgotify has been invented to play only sounds provided through the online streaming service Spotify that have never been previously chosen or heard by anyone.

To rescue recordings from obscure somnolence, an entire social world has to be stimulated, or, if necessary, defilibrated into existence — word-of-mouth agitated through a battery of strategically deployed distractions: buzz, hype, public relations, profit motives, payola, gossip, press, celebrity, image, star power, controversy — all this in the hope of drawing listeners to the megabytes, the vinyl, the discs or the tapes, and perhaps, with some luck, even beyond that to the actual producer or musician.

• • •

The model of a less cluttered conduit between composer and listener, of composing directly to a sound storage mechanism, might well feel relatively straightforward and unproblematic for composers working within Eurological parameters, such as Schaeffer or James Tenney, as, for them, electronic means would simply offer an alternative to monological performance for the construction and presentation of sonorous objects.

However, the studio's accumulated abilities to alter recorded sound also introduces a metacommunicational ambiguity between its seemingly documentary persona and direct studio invention that can veer toward what the French cultural theorist Jean Baudrillard celebrated as simulacra, representations of "realities" that haven't actually "happened." When one listens to a recording, how much of what one is hearing attempts to accurately depict musicians' actions and how much compositional "enhancement" has been added by the producer. In other words, just *whom* is one listening to?

In the 1970s, more than 20 years after Les Paul's first overdubbed recordings, Rahsaan Roland Kirk, who could think and play as many as four wind instruments simultaneously, having been recast as an unwilling John Henry, would occasionally stop in the middle of a set to rail against studio tricks that mocked and devalued his own very substantive musical capacities and achievements. Just what good is what appeared to be his artistry when it could be so easily "simulated" in a studio?

Nevertheless, if a new tool becomes available, why shouldn't people use it? Why shouldn't they see what it can do? After all, Adolphe Sax couldn't have anticipated Coleman Hawkins or Albert Ayler, not to mention Rahsaan.

• • •

Regardless, both musician and producer share a common interest in their recorded emissaries' capacity to withstand and entice repeated listenings, and they really do have some serious work cut out for them. Eno's talk may have stressed how listening to a recording over and over yields new insights and recognitions, but witnessing this sort of rote repetition equally exposes faults, weaknesses and errors.

At their best, musicians might respond to this with the single "perfect" take that they already aspire to in live performance. But, producers, in contrast, are positioned to take advantage of the post-production options of "improving," "sweetening" or substantially reconfiguring the recorded sonic object, which very differently situates compositional options and opportunities.

This dissimilarity of access and perspective yields contrasting priorities and behaviors. For musicians, studio assemblages can function as valuable documentary samples for listeners or as maquettes for further musical experiment and activity, but for the studio producer, the recorded artifact identifies the final target of all imaginings and efforts.

Composition *for musicians*, whether monologically or dialogically organized, is explicitly *social*. Both are specifically designed to affect people, to direct and/or influence the actions of collaborating players. In this sense, a monological composer's function might be analogized with a playwright's, while the relations among musicians, conductors and dialogical composers share at least a few parallels with theater directors and actors.

A producer, however, operates more like a film director who may invite, or even provoke, a wealth of collaboration and dialogical interaction. But, once these scenes have been "shot," subsequent decisions no longer concern compositional social relations at all (save with an imagined eventual listener), but only issues of design and sound quality. A producer "plays" and alters gathered sounds as a musician would navigate an instrument, an ensemble or a compositional interface.

But, this is an instrument that plays more retroactive than active, more easily disposed toward a historian's, curator's or editor's amendments than the initiatives of actor, author or musician. The tools of the sound studio facilitate an assemblage of fragmentary instances, core likewise to cinematic production, toward a verisimilitude convincing enough for presentation to the experiential time of listening.

• • •

It shouldn't surprise, then, that the recording process has always dictated some terms of engagement to performers. For example, this technology was initially unable to assimilate the sonorous fullness of percussion instruments and therefore kept them at bay. Early acetate disc capacity additionally imposed upon musicians the discipline of the three minute statement. One may even further speculate as to whether the eventual displacement of the bass viol by the bass guitar was because its considerably simpler overtone profile could be heard more easily through the spectrum available to the amplitude modulation projecting through car radios.

Decorative stagings such as Phil Spector's anthemic auditorium ambiences aside, the decisive compositional shifts favoring producers over musicians accelerated in the late 1960s with more sophisticated multitrack recording, which inspired the Beatles to, like Glen Gould, forego live performance completely, and, with producer George Martin, instead dedicate months to discovering and assembling new sonic imagery layer by layer for eventual release in a sedimentary accumulation of incremental composings from the inside out.

Within just a few years of this breakthrough, much studio procedure had begun to "rationalize" sound construction in a manner most kin with the assembly line concepts systematically advanced by Henry Ford early in the 20th century. Ford dispensed with earlier team approaches, where a group of workers would together assemble a vehicle from start to finish, in favor of a more efficient atomization of labor, with each worker, in sequential isolation, contributing to no more than a single step of the total assembly, perhaps just screwing in one particular bolt, over and over, day after day.

With an adequate budget, a producer might likewise call on a long line of choice musicians, each of whom could record an individual track in addition to what had already been recorded without any necessary personal or compositional interaction. This is a procedure that almost recalls Mel Brook's "cone of silence" from his 1960s television spoof on the U.S. national "security" apparatus, *Get Smart*. Two spies could confer within this privacy assurance device without being overheard. The catch was that they couldn't hear each other either.

Sequential overdubbing likewise obscures musician access to a music's composite sound. That perspective has been reserved to the producer. Compositional agency migrates from intra-musician syntheses to the control booth. Dialogical information's exponential complexity is circumvented for a much simpler and more manageable monological current. There are some solid justifications for this too. If the goal is to assemble the "best" possible sonorous product, absolute separation of component tracks facilitates the finest degree of producer control in crafting an eventually issued sonic image.

• • •

This method of assemblage doesn't operate anything like a gospel, jazz (or kindred) rhythm section, where time communications are not strictly metronomic or quantized. Each player is encircled — as each encircles the others — within webs of mutual influence. Each sound played refinesses the motions being articulated. What might seem a steady, "objective" pulse has actually to be discovered and continually renegotiated in process. There might be slight, or even radical, shifts of tempo, accent, weight and rhythm as response along with the ongoing evolution of the music. Growth and unpredictability are unavoidably endemic to these relations.

This sort of reciprocal irregularity evolves as a simultaneous whole that can't be segmented into discrete parts even though separate instruments and players are involved. Sequentially layered studio recording therefore demanded some adaptation from musicians.

For example, many experienced drummers initially struggled when asked to lay down a first basic track for subsequent overdubbing in conjunction with nothing other than a click track, which is a studio metronome.

Unlike a fellow musician, a metronome isn't at all interested, and won't ever become interested, bored, annoyed or inspired. Response or invention simply doesn't appear within this lexicon. But then, click tracks have never been intended to feed musicians ideas or impulses, but only to establish a predictable reference for each successively added track. Each new track may record a reaction to what's already been recorded, but what's recorded will never answer the musician who's playing. Multitracking in this way accumulates layers of unidirectionally directed soliloquies to what eventually consolidates into a closed system as a "fixed" musical "work."

The click track, later transformed into a default setting via computerized quantization of tempo, introduces into music what Gullah-Geechie polyrhythmicist and scholar David Pleasant has aptly termed "clone time" (a musical analogue to the genetic modification of biological organisms), where each pulse is, down to the millisecond, precisely and consistently equidistant.

One might hear this as a musically unprecedented tethering of reciprocal human variability to impersonal, non-responsive measure, although, technically, a producer *could* opt to micromanage each pulse interval for more affective nuance and verisimilitude. But then, just how would one determine monologically such fluctuations, which, among musicians emerges relationally? The mathematics of *that* by itself would most likely wax overwhelming. And, how could that temporal plasticity be as effectively generated through, say, an algorithm when there's actually no *story* happening among these pulses in the first place?

Click tracks distinctively contradict the everyday experience that no two human repetitions are, in actual practice, precisely identical. Organic, responsorial repetition is indefinitely permeable to complexes of circumstance. A producer's alternative to clone patterns throughout a construction would, understandably, given that it's an awful lot less work, seem irresistible. Besides, who's going to notice, and who'd care anyway? The easy opportunities afforded by the studio are no less predictive than any other compositional context.

. . .

With a toolkit substantially augmented by synthesizers, samplers and software, the potential roles of a producer/studio composer have since expanded from that of intermediary between musicians and remote audiences to self-contained, autonomous compositional agents in their own right. This development repositions musicians as only one of many possible means to an end (at the very least, from a producer's perspective), as decorative, if not totally disposable, accessories, possibly useful here and there for an extra cameo bit of spice, but not in any way conceptually, formally or sonically necessary.

A producer-centric milieu opens to a post-musician soundscape. Within this context, musician generated sound begins to resemble some quaint, artisanal speciality like locally produced organic cheeses, craft beers and whiskeys, hand-crafted woodwork and jewelry for small, niche coteries. What had not very long before embodied how music of the people happened has been reconfigured into an elective indulgence.

Aside from the "abstract" electronic sound that goes well beyond what musicians and instruments could accomplish, the large majority of post-musician studio production, ironically, still seems most to paraphrase musician performance, although often hardly anybody's home anymore. Rather than departing radically from earlier models, the positions of drummer, bassist, harmony and melody instruments continue, more often than not, to be emulated, although usually these sounds no longer correspond with any exchanges among compositional agents.

It falls primarily upon a producer's curatorial acumen (with or without overdubbed musician recordings) to combine enough peak instances, with just the right mix, EQ and ambient tracks to convincingly simulate the heat, life, ignition and combustion of a great dialogical band on fire. But that's not actually what the sounds portray. What's instead delivered is a monologically coordinated sonic hyper-reality.

Ghosts & Specters

Recordings do more than enlighten and preserve, they cast shadows. In oral, non-alphabetic cultures, musical sound is often inextricable from interrelations with the more-than-human environment. Everyone musicks, so much so that music as a dedicated sound art might not even be distinguished at all from other activities. Some, like Christopher Small, have argued that 20th century musical education in European dominated cultures (his experience was primarily in England) has succeeded in shaming many ordinary people out of musicking altogether, as their amateur enjoyment failed to immediately measure up to professional standards.

Before recordings became available, most middle class families in the Americas and Europe owned pianos, and somebody in each house had to be playing one, player pianos aside. Those with fewer disposable resources didn't let that stop them from generating their own musical sound either. Recordings, however presented the first possibility of enjoying musical sound without people having to generate musical sound themselves, and, even more profoundly, the possibility of musical sound *without* people at all.

The extraordinarily convenient access recording affords to musical sounds from any place, and from a wide variety of pasts, far outshines some intrinsic, often unstated caveats. Recordings encourage an illusion that all musics are somehow "the same" in that these preserved sonic images are themselves "the music," whereas these musics are also so much more than their sounds alone and are far more variegated than the sounds all by themselves can convey. Sounds present evidence and sensation but they are not, neither in themselves nor by themselves, the event — or the story.

• • •

The recorded abstraction of sounds from their music also introduces musical sound as "product" and listener as consumer. It doesn't have to be like this. Listening is a mode of composition itself, of putting sounds together, of making one's own "sense" of sounds, but it needn't be solipsistic or solely indulgent. With just a bit of imagination and curiosity, recorded sounds can be heard as the bridges they also are.

In Spanish, the words *ensayo* (to assay, or test) and *repetición* (repetition) can designate "rehearsal," which in its antecedent French forms also indicated "repetition," although the sense of "to hear again" is hard not to draw from the contemporary English formation of *re-hear-sal*.

Recordings can facilitate a kind of rehearsal of listening. A recording may repeat verbatim, but listening may "hear" and compose something more each time. This saturating repetition, rich in potential revelation of detail, can help to better season listeners for live listening to actual music as it happens.

Although recordings can ably document sequential histories of music, their reductionism, at the same time, can flatten a listener's estimation of time-space. It doesn't matter when or where they were recorded, recorded sounds encounter listeners only within an immediate present. "Old" and "new" play equally contemporary when prerecorded.

A 70 year old recording may deliver new, ear opening experience and epiphanies to a 15 year old. Historical distinctions only become practical and meaningful when initiating one's own musical sounds, although the boundary of the contemporary has grown a much fuzzier signal to noise ratio than formerly. Recordings repeatedly verify the sounds of past moments, which would otherwise have been lost, if not forgotten, with the potential of unlimited repetition.

...

As sonic monuments, recordings of extraordinary musicians long gone may tower intimidatingly over current musicians who may always feel diminished in their shadow, no matter how much these documents might have to teach. One might find oneself in creative competition with not only one's living contemporaries, but, more than ever, with every musician ever recorded, although the reality is that any artist can only respond within one's own current means and circumstances.

The acute presentness of a recording also tends to downplay that sonic images of the past can't be known or lived the way they actually were because, for the most part, they emerged out of contexts that no longer exist and can't be replicated. A great deal of archeological translation and transposition has to be achieved to meaningfully transform one's comprehension from third person description into first person application.

The lost-in-translation effect graphically shows itself where musicians faithfully emulate what they've heard on recordings in a belief that absolute sonic resemblance to a recorded model is all there is to the art — or to art, period. What they can't immediately hear (because it can only be, at most, inferred from a recording) are the experiments and the mistakes, the seeking and the revision, the aspirations, dreams, intentions and disputes. What a musician might apprehend as a fixed "style" to be adopted as a badge of orthodoxy might actually have been only a single phase in a longer, far more uncertain developmental process.

One finally has to determine for oneself whether the *way* of a music (*how* an artist proceeds: with what attitudes and values) are to be more fundamental to what one does, or — are the surface symptoms ("style," or the *what*) of a music to be the primary focus of one's activity. Is one's art to enable more "verb" (where the outcome may hover yet to be discovered) or "noun" (where action orients toward a preordained destination)? Is a music to pose questions, or is it to presuppose an answer?

Sometimes recordings can, perhaps inadvertently, function as rebuke. In 2000, Jazz at Lincoln Center programmed a number of presentations in celebration of Louis Armstrong's centennial. Among these was a free concert for young listeners, where the opening set featured a live performance by Winton Marsalis and cohorts playing in early 20th century New Orleans style. The rapport with the young audience plus adults was considerate and engagingly cordial, the playing ably, elegantly and unimpeachably "correct."

Sequel to this was some Edward R. Murrow produced black and white footage from 1956 of Louis Armstrong and His All Stars playing live in Accra, soon to be capital of a nominally liberated Ghana. The 44 year old celluloid decidedly outplayed the living and breathing musicians still present in the room. In contrast with Marsalis &

company's deliberately retrospective emulations, Armstrong's band, without a doubt, had clearly intended to rock the house, to lift the bandstand in the manner of James Brown, Aretha Franklin or the John Coltrane Quartet, whereas the initial set, strong as it may have been *formally*, projected more of the respectful politeness one might expect from a Euroclassical string quartet. If, during that first set, had the musicians played as if *their own* lives actually depended on it, as did the All Stars, in terms of the questions and uncertainties of their *personally* lived experience, likely their music would have sounded different than it did.

Flipping the Archival

During dance parties in the Bronx in the early 1970s, DJ Kool Herc (Clive Campbell) discovered how to transform the vinyl phonographic disc and turntable into a musical instrument through the merry-go-round technique (alternating turntables to enact a continuous sonic loop), subverting the recorded artifact by rendering it contingent upon the live recontextualization of the DJ, which is to say, composing from the inside out. Jeff Chang, in his *Can't Stop Won't Stop* history of hip-hop, recounts that the supplanting of live musicians with DJs had initially developed in Campbell's native Jamaica.

> According to dance-hall historian Norman Stolzoff, sound system culture had evolved in Kingston after World War II when the ranks of live musicians dramatically thinned due to immigration to the United Kingdom and the United States and the rise of the North Coast tourist industry. By the time (Lee "Scratch") Perry came to Kingston, sound systems had largely replaced bands.

Within less than a decade of Kool Herc's innovation, Reaganomics enthusiastically began gutting the public education programs in the arts and music that had for decades opened access for working class people (many of whom were African American) to high levels of instrumental musicianship and knowledge. But, in place of that, inexpensive electronic devices, such as drum machines, sequencers and synthesizers, were becoming available, and people appropriated and utilized these emerging alternatives alongside this repurposing of the turntable.

Turntabilism evolved into a sophisticated improvisational language where multiple sound sources (a variety of discs mixed and juxtaposed from two turntables) can be collaged live into a unique and personal sound. The incorporation of scratching by Grand Wizard Theodore and Grandmaster Flash not so long after Herc's breakthrough, where record needle turns percussive sound generator, pushed the turntable irreversibly past its initial recitation propensities into a distinctive and autonomous musical instrument, and the developing lexicon of turntable moves has since continued to develop and expand.

Turntabilism's manipulation of prerecorded sound sources also anticipated the later evolution of sampling. Composition through sampling initially approaches sound bodies at far lower levels of resolution than do most musician/composers. This is because so much of a music's compositional decisions have already been determined (an example of compositional decision at close to maximum grain might be one's choice of a track from a playlist). Via sampling, higher resolution compositional decisions, such as an original Clyde Stubblefield drum break, might be extracted whole without having oneself to go through the experiments, questions and technical developments that the percussionist ventured (what, once upon a time, would have been referred to as part of "paying dues") to invoke that particular sound body.

A turntablist's compositional invention, like a producer's, instead emerges in the transformation and recontextualization of adopted source material, somewhat the way an arranger might recast a given sonic design. But, it also, in a way, resembles conduction, as neither conductionalist nor turntabilist generate or invent the initial sounds they redirect. Both have to act and decide compositionally exactly as the sound is emerging, immediately exposed to listener attention, rather than wait to later "fix it in the mix," as a producer could. Turntabilism not only projectively composes from the inside out, its compositional streams develop dialogically, as they did during its countervoice to the MC prominence in earlier hip-hop, and continue to do with fellow sonic agents and dancers.

Instrument

Nothing would be recorded at all were it not for a microphone. Like the *micro*-scope, the *micro*-phone brings into perceptible range what couldn't be noticed otherwise. The destination of a microphone's signal, when not feeding directly into a recording, channels toward amplification. And, the most immediate effect on musical sound that amplification introduces is not necessarily how it can increase volume, but its diversification of possible timbres and timbral combinations.

With amplification, the guitar string can tandem with a trumpet, singers needn't restrict their delivery to belting, a flute may comfortably solo with a rhythm section. And, beyond the amplified acoustic instrument, electronic instruments themselves, such as the ondes martenot, the theramin and the analog synthesizer, were each invented as much in pursuit of new and more flexible timbres as toward any other possibility.

What all amplified instruments share is their transmission of sounds through loudspeakers. Loudspeakers are sonically flexible chameleons. They can project just about anything one throws at them. This generalist propensity contrasts with the far more limiting specificities of wood, brass, animal skin or gut, horsehair, reeds, platinum, bamboo or gourds. Ironically, speakers may often, nevertheless, generate sound with reduced, rather than greater, complexity.

• • •

A speaker projects sound from a single point, whereas the sound emanating from a cello, for example, is far more irregular, and that irregularity sculpts a tactilely noticeable quality of experience. The sound at the bridge differs from that at the F-holes, or the bass bar, or the end pin, the scroll, the fingerboard. The front sounds different from the back, which sounds different from the left or right, above or below, near or far.

All of these contrastingly resonating areas then spread discontinuously into the variations of the surrounding acoustic environment. Each point within the polydirectional sphere one listens is differently inflected, all together accumulating a distinctively palpable dimensionality.

Then, add to this the varying pressures, touch, attack and sustain each individual cellist might contribute to that composite sound. Consider also the acoustic complexity of a trap set, the fine grades across each area of a cymbal chosen with the highly informed deliberation of a connoisseur, the sticks, the tuning of each head, the varying sonorities of each zone of that skin.

• • •

That both electronic instruments and recordings approach listeners by way of the loudspeaker, reveals a common acoustic disposition. One of the transformative effects of recording on listening is that recorded and speaker projected sound have, in an art-influences-life (or, maybe tech-influences-life) fashion, come to set the acoustic standard even for much live performance.

At an Edgard Varèse two night retrospective series of concerts presented at Avery Fisher Hall in 2010, there was an opportunity to witness his 3 dimensional electronic construction *Poème Électronique* as one could never hear it through headphones, in stereo or quadraphonic surround-sound. During the performance afterwards of some of his earlier, more chamber scale constructions, one could almost be persuaded that one was instead listening to the recording one remembers instead of live musicians.

The sound of the violin in particular, seemed uncannily flat, lacking the fragility it ordinarily inherits from wood and bow. Eventually it became more evident that each instrument was being microphoned and piped through a sound system in this high-end concert hall designed for world class acoustics. And then, there are legends of famous pop stars lip syncing live with their own recordings. All's well so long as, um, technical difficulties don't intrude.

What speakers lack in acoustic complexity (a more ambitious electronic musician might try the more expensive and cumbersome option of coordinating a number of differently oriented speakers) can be compensated for by volume. When amplified to deafness promoting thresholds, sound begins to be experienced even more in bones, body fluids and muscles than though ears alone as it impresses an almost aquatic or amniotic intimacy.

Recordings are similarly vulnerable. A recording by an old school crew such as Public Enemy booms with the depth of Chuck

D's extraordinary voice when pumped as loud as it's intended to be, but if played softly in the kitchen on a little boom box it begins, despite itself, to resemble karaoke. One hears what sounds like someone in a booth rhyming along with what seems a prerecorded background. Pop on some headphones and the resonance of the skull restores the vital sensation (or is this always an illusion?) of sonic mass.

• • •

One's principal musical instrument is, regardless, always one's own body. What else would it be? This is where sensation, awareness, intention and imagination happen. A musical actor has to cultivate self-synchrony: coordinating ears, imagination, breath, hands, mouth, throat, feet, reflexes, alertness, flexibility. And, in that regard, the U.S./Ghanaian musicologist Kofi Agawu has even challenged the stereotype of Euroclassical musicians as lacking rhythm by pointing out the rhythmic complexity of the physical coordination involved in just playing a violin at all, regardless of how redundantly four-squared the sonic design might be.

Each instrument exerts its own particular cost. Its peculiar resistance characterizes its sound. Its restrictions identify the specificity of its locale, its palpable reality. The same design voiced on a trumpet presents a very different physical experience to a player than it would on a keyboard, clarinet or guitar. This physicality, this combined positioning of fingers, lips, diaphragm, back, neck, foot, hip becomes, on each respective instrument, part of the concept and experience of that sound. One's conception is not only of the sound in isolation, but also of the lived dance that releases it.

Those who play electronic instruments can verify that the time and effort dedicated to developing spontaneous fluency is no less than with any acoustic instrument. Nevertheless, it's always unclear just how much *any* instrument plays the player, whether the absence of overt muscularity or breath in playing, say, a laptop, for example, speaks directly enough to the body, or leads to more detached, more impersonalized or automated music, or whether it overly diffuses or obscures personal identity.

• • •

Virtuosity with acoustic instruments is problematic enough. Being able to whiz through fast or difficult passages doesn't necessarily mean a musician has anything to say yet. Regardless of a musician's facility, the fundamental question of *why this sound rather than that sound* never really goes away. This doesn't exactly mean that the unexamined sound isn't worth playing either, as exploratory playing is itself sonic examination, but it does mean that virtuosity comes with more than technical responsibilities. The peak virtuosities of Art Tatum, Dizzy Gillespie, Elvin Jones or Evan Parker didn't evolve from "talent" but from imagination fueled hunger. Technique is only one of many possible answers to such a hunger; and without that, technique founders in posing an answer that's yet to discover its questions.

Any instrument, simply in presenting a distinct entity, bounds relationship through its predispositions. It imposes its own presets. For example, modern European instruments, for the most part, are more or less preset for A-440 tempered intonation. Software generated presets for an electronic instrument are of another order, however, in that they additionally preset "content" averaged by software engineers through compromises such as MIDI.

Presets may offer a substitute instant virtuosity, not only uninvented and potentially unexamined by the composer, but supplied at such quantity that no person could, at least within spontaneous circumstances, cognitively process and evaluate the material in order to consistently transform them into earned, personalized compositional choices. Presets prejudice the possible and potentially circumscribe imagination before it's even had a chance to get started. The fare for fast leapfrogging over human limits might be leaving out most of what's human.

However, composer and trombonist George Lewis, for example, rather than adopting a computer as a mechanical receptacle of commands or complying with whatever built-in default tendencies, has developed his own sound generation software that interacts with the inputs and decision streams of an improviser, that reflects and alters, that talks back and challenges a dialogical composer and continually expands upon the implications of that composer's invention in a multidimensionalizing of the individual's presence and action. He accepts the options and opportunities of the technology while respecting its own identity and agency in specifically animist terms.

Soundscape

Industrialism has encouraged among many people a deafness to water. Without water, there'd be no human consciousness at all. About 100 pounds of a person who weighs 150 pounds is water on a planet with a surface that's about 71% water covered. The German researcher Theodor Schwenk has documented water's acute susceptibility for conveying information.

Water flow patterns register such less than visible influences as the Earth's rotation, gravity, topography, temperature and electromagnetic variation. Among Schwenk's "drop-pictures" are enlarged images of drips falling into fresh spring water that radiate leaf-like vortices from the point of impact in well articulated, nearly symmetrical, flower-like patterns in contrast with other samples of chemically treated and polluted water that reverberate far less integrated, even disorganized, configurations.

People who have to carry their household water some distance would likely recognize water quite a bit differently than would a more hothouse cultivated person who'd be more inclined to let it run mindlessly out of a tap as if nothing were really there, without a thought of where it comes from, not to mention of watersheds, hydrologic cycles, aquifers, scarcity, preciousness or sacredness.

Recording's sleight of hand ability to affect renunciation of its own sources, to deliver musical sound without listeners actually having to deal with, or even acknowledge, other people (such as musicians or producers) in order to hear it, its apparent emulation of immaculate conception, positions it as the tap water of music. Recordings never tire. Their hardware might run down, but recordings themselves never need to take breaks or eat. They feel no mercy. In fact, they don't feel anything at all.

A hyperabundance of recorded sound at everyone's fingertips on command doesn't necessarily mean that more relationship with musical sound will develop, or that people will listen more closely or that they'll imagine more broadly. It doesn't block that either. But, there's also a slippery slope to overload that can easily default musical sound to ornament, ear candy, filler, imaginary friend, imaginary pet, aural carpeting, decoration, narcotic, or soundtrack to one's whims. These selective functions, useful as they might be for some on occasion, necessarily insulate themselves through indifference, through disinclinations to hear very far beyond routine habit. The notion that musical sound might also act as living interface among people, that it might demonstrate people with minds, sensibilities and reasons runs instead unnoticed and straight down the drain.

• • •

Sound's zero-sum characteristics unavoidably mess with thresholds of consent. Quiet can't fight noise. The loud invincibly overwhelms the crepuscular. Consensually amplitude-intensified musical sound can define a physical location that distinguishes a sonic commonality and might even in that way invite community. But, absent this consent, amplitude converts sound to weaponry. Its blanket obliteration of low profile sound and communication confirms its unwillingness to listen as it bullies the vulnerable and the sleepless.

High volume musical sound, however, may also retaliate as self-defense, resistance, affirmation and celebration — especially for those people structurally endangered, silenced, left out or otherwise slated for invisibility. Where muzak and recorded messages incessantly trail people already inundated by sounds of traffic and other mechanized activity, in soundscapes so abjectly abandoned by quiet, recorded sound fortifies a territorial defense strategy against the impersonal intrusions of sonic imposition.

Headphones and ear buds allow the sounds a listener loves to follow wherever one goes. One's personal choice of sound no longer has to intrude at all into neighboring soundscapes, and no one need disagree nor feel disturbed. Sounds may be kept confidential, even secret, as listening has slipped almost entirely away from the social into an exclusive and preprogrammed privacy.

Sounds, surprises and happenings outside the portable recording merely slip past notice and seem to lose magnetism and importance. A sonically public world, even where a musician might happen to be playing on a subway platform, might even be regarded as unwanted and annoying intrusion. A school bus once upon a time resounding with raucous youth can, with enough devices and headphones, hush right up like a library.

• • •

Hearing is tactile. One is literally touched by vibrating air. The air, which envelops us inside and outside, is also literally skin. One feels the near and the distant through this both invisible and fluid exterior as sound. Hearing can, of course, contend with brisk cut and massive pounce, but it's also able to discern minutely among caresses, whispers, brushes, hints, pauses, insinuations — and this is the range of hearing that the multiple drones of industrial/post-industrial noisescapes drown out first.

Prior to noisescape's dominion, the most subtle of sounds could scout the distant outposts of consciousness. Environment could be perceived through sound as if part of one's own internal proprioception. One could sonically perceive activities situated miles away as well as tiny, incremental motion nearby.

Sound recordist Gordon Hempton has found only one soundscape in the contiguous United States as of yet thoroughly unaltered by human generated sound (aircraft, not recorded sound, being its most pervasive and penetrating broadcaster) that he's marked with a small red stone in the Hoh Rainforest deep within Olympic National Park at the northwest corner of the state of Washington, a spot he endeavors to protect through his One Square Inch of Silence project.

In *The Spell of the Sensuous*, ecologist/philosopher David Abram suggests that, before the diffusion of phonetic writing (sound notation), people literally read (decoded, interpreted) their actual environs — the landscape, the water, the air, the vegetation and animals, the "more-than-human world" — as their "text." All were considered sentient agents in their own right, each with their own distinctive epistemologies.

While pictorial scripts, at the least, included images of the environment's denizens in their depiction of words and ideas, thus retaining, to an extent, reminders of reciprocal interconnectedness, phonetic writing needed only to notate human pronunciation. Nothing beyond the immediately human remained absolutely necessary. This, Abram argues, precipitated an intellectual withdrawal from the real world into the abstraction of anthropocentrism, into a self-referential, exclusively human identity, where the rest of the actual world no longer spoke and became dumb. There was no longer anyone there to listen to.

Notated language presents some formidable technology. So does sound recording. Recording remembers, but it also quite persuasively forgets and obscures. It's highly valuable conveyance, but it's *not* music. That task of re-membering falls to listeners, whose imaginations have to restore what recording leaves out as well as what it can't tell.

19

The Sociality of Rhythm

God's Eye View

The parameters of sound most commonly cited are duration, frequency, amplitude, timbre and, sometimes, morphology. Where sound acts as hub, body, hinge and image, as it does in music, what stands out most here is that rhythm is absent from these designated properties of "sounds in themselves." The implication is that rhythm is extrasonic, that the vibrations that constitute sounds resonate from activities that might otherwise be silent, unheard and unrecognized.

Sound in itself may occasion experience, but it is also symptom, and possibly signal. It's both body and intermediary. Sound's source is action, change, movement, difference, friction. And while recurrent patterns of movement may range among the cosmic, microbiological, geological or subatomic, the perceivers of these rhythms (therefore part of a rhythm's generation) are those who recognize them as such. This is also to say that listeners "music" sounds.

This actuality provided a basis for John Cage's arguments on behalf of an abolition of music. He asserted rightly that any sound can be listened to musically, that each listener may compose a music to one's own ears from whatever soundscape might be presenting itself. This opportunity has always been available to anyone willing to notice it, so, to that extent, he's reissued what could be a perennial wake up call. He angled further that listeners should behold "sounds in themselves" as aesthetically autonomous entities, disabused of any associations with their context or origins; again, something anyone can do anytime and not really dependent on whether people actively generate musical sound or not.

On behalf of unfettered sounds being heard as "music," Cage sought to purge human musical sound generation of human intention. He devised theatrically laborious methods of organizing compositional decisions through chance driven methodologies in order to transcend the biases of personal likes and dislikes and to "liberate" sound from human projected meanings and mannerisms.

Having, with exceptional wit, cleverness and invention made his point, Cage also affirmed the complete pointlessness of musical activity: if all and any sounds present "equal" musicality, then the act of generating sounds for listeners turns no more than distractingly redundant and superfluous. His work proposes a totally listenercentric soniverse that hints at a gated community nostalgia for the posthuman, for a purity of soundscapes untainted by human entanglements, for what the poet Robert Duncan once humorously critiqued as a "god's eye view."

As composer, Cage embraced this pointlessness of musical activity with the support of his interpretations of Zen Buddhism. If his incorporation of Zen sensibility might have been less touristic, one could have expected him to, like Zen masters of yore, to have withdrawn from everyday society to a remote hut in the mountains where he could serenely embrace the ecstatic roar of all things. Instead he went public and prolific, gradually reaping the institutional benefits sometimes bestowed upon composers within the pan-European monological tradition, within which he played the avant-gardist role of loyal opposition: both internal dissenter and external defender.

Although packaged in a disarmingly affable persona, Cage was both dismissive and patronizing toward African American dialogical music. As far as music was concerned, his anarchist sympathies for freedom and self determination extended to listeners but not quite so far as those actors who imagine and sound music. In the sequel to his groundbreaking and influential book *Silence, A Year from Monday*, Cage opined:

> Music as discourse (jazz)
> doesn't work.
> If you're going to have a discussion.
> have it, and use words.

The didactic authority of this pronouncement appears to slosh among some half-baked ambiguities. One could ask, where Cage selects the word "discourse," why didn't he indicate, say, motivic development instead, which has been so fundamental to centuries of pan-European (as well as other) musical practices which "discuss" a particular sonic pattern. And, when he says, "doesn't work;" doesn't work for whom? Doesn't work for what? No clue.

Discussion and dialogue are not exactly identical, but Cage might have been objecting to multipersonic, dialogical composition on principle. Musical sound marked by recognizable traces of compositional personae is at variance with his own desire to efface the appearance of personal agency within music. And, although in many ways attracted to organizational decentralization, Cage may have also taken issue with the music's compositional social structure itself, especially as it both evolved outside the pan-European tradition and challenged the hegemony of monological organization.

George Lewis, in his comprehensive and carefully nuanced 2002 essay, *Improvised Music after 1950: Afrological and Eurological Perspectives,* points out that, about five to eight years after the emergence of bebop, some Euroclassicist composers began to respond to the possible solutions dialogical procedures demonstrated regarding impasses within their own tradition, but without openly acknowledging the source. He quotes Anthony Braxton's *Triaxium Writings*, "Both aleatory and indeterminism are words which have been coined . . . to bypass the word improvisation and as such the influence of non-white sensibility."

Cage may have tried to square the circle of maintaining the cultural hierarchy of Eurological practices over others (which corresponds with the colonial inheritance of white privilege in both Europe and the Americas) while attempting to incorporate regenerative innovations from artists historically relegated by violence, law, hypocrisy and custom to second class social status. In departure from the stable sonic imagery previously sought through monological methodologies, Cage activated performances where exactly which sounds happen becomes unforeseen, variable, indeterminate, and therefore, each time intrinsically experimental and unique.

Of course, formalist engagement with the unforeseen had already been frequenting bandstands in Harlem, on 52nd street and beyond for quite a while, but it seems that Cage preferred maintaining the unidirectional compositional relationships characteristic of monological organization's propensity for presenting musical sounds as strictly autonomous sonic objects. His solution to this dilemma proposed an artifactual indeterminacy that initiates unpredictable sonic events while (in contrast with dialogical procedures) prohibiting any compositional *response* to these unforeseens.

"Bad politics make good art," Cage once wrote, "but of what use is good art?" Through an insistence on monological structure, even if liberalized and finessed with deliberately vague indications, this often innovative composer conveniently sidestepped some of musical composition's core structural challenges in relation to information flow and communication by appearing to assume that they don't really exist.

Cage's cake-and-eat-it-too espousal of an agentless music (where chance determines his compositions but for which he still takes credit) is problematic in other ways. Disavowal of agency edges close to anonymity, not the absence of celebrity once enjoyed by some artists in medieval Europe, but the impunity conferred through the anonymity of authority. It's possible that Cage could afford to affect such "disappearance" because his features, complexion and educational background (symbols of an emperor's-new-clothes transcendence of "history" and "memory") in themselves didn't immediately threaten his day to day access to a reasonably unimpeded and full existence.

Accordingly, he could, with little challenge, concur with those social/aesthetic boundaries that have coded Eurological music variously as "serious," "experimental," "new," "art," "concert," "avant-garde," "composed" or "contemporary" as if none of these terms could ever have applied to Charlie Parker or any others outside its self-designated loop, a genteel sort of aesthetic, interpersonal and access-to-resource apartheid that has yet to mature into healthy pluralism.

Cage's thought is nevertheless worth contending with because his contributions to music are far enough from trivial. His work challenges anyone who encounters it to not take for granted one's own conceptions and preconceptions of musical possibility. More than anyone else, he broke down the conventional barriers between "musical" and "non-musical" sound, and his ideas and example have found application and influence well beyond the practice of music. His cultivation, especially with choreographer Merce Cunningham, of non-interfering simultaneities demonstrates (likely "without intention") an important expansion of the constructive principles of polyrhythm.

He also proffers a solid critique of the impact of rhythm on musical sound. If sounds are being asked to function as Duchampian found objects, the perceptual gravities of rhythm tend to subsume sounds within an externally imposed matrix of emphases and deemphases that distracts listeners from each sound's intrinsic morphology. And he does have a point. Perpetual insistence on the arbitrary imposition of a beat, regardless of the character of other participating sounds, impoverishes the far wider range of rhythms that can be felt and recognized.

Cage's deliberate, stopwatch parceled arhythmics also counterpose the unavoidable rhythmic propensities of his all too human audiences. Repeated listening to a recording of any random sonic event can elicit identifications of pattern and interconnection. And, as one begins to condense and generalize a sense of shape, sequence and progression, one may also engage in rhythms of anticipation and proportionate comparison. The tendency to group sounds into distinctive identities with beginnings, middles and ends begins to punctuate a soundscape with rhythmic markings. And, even an unprecedented listening may map itself against other hearings of the same sort and friction some sort of responsive pulsation. One can become so accustomed to randomness that it might acquire an acceptably dronelike continuity all its own.

Microbeats

"If you're going to have a discussion, have it, and use words." Cage may well have insisted on words, but one of his coevals, the anthropologist Edward T. Hall, was suggesting at the same time that as much as 90% of human communication is non-verbal. Hall began his work in the 1930s, emphasizing friendship (in sharp contrast with other more "disinterested" anthropological procedures) as his primary approach to participant observation. He initiated intercultural communication as a formal area of study, studies of non-verbal communication — as in the case of what he came to call *proxemics* (interpersonal spatial distance as a language of social communication), studies of cultural notions of interactive time and his conceptualization of technology as an amplification or extension of the human body, a notion foundationally influential on one of Cage's own favorite thinkers, Marshall McLuhan.

"Viewed in the context of human behavior, time is organization." wrote Hall in his 1983 *The Dance of Life*, where he discussed the findings of William Condon, a researcher trained in kinesics, philosophy (with a special interest in phenomenology) and psychology, who coined the term *entrainment*: "the process that occurs when two or more people become engaged in each other's rhythms."

Condon spent a year and a half (four to five hours a day) in the 1960s studying 4 1/2 seconds of Professor Gregory Bateson's film of a family eating dinner. He wore out 130 copies of this 4 1/2 second sequence. Each copy weathered 100,000 viewings.

Condon used sophisticated time-motion analysis to "identify the building blocks used in the organization of human behavior" and discovered correlations between components of speech, the body's accompanying microgestures and brain wave frequencies, a coordination of a person with one's own rhythms that Hall refers to as *self-synchrony*. Hall focuses briefly on a single nine word, one second long, phase spoken in the film clip:

> During this one second the subject's arm is precisely coordinated with the theta wave pattern; her eye blinks are in sync with the beta wave pattern; the alpha rhythm is in sync with the words or vice versa. Condon states: "These basic rhythms seem to become part of the very being of the person. ...His whole body participates in that rhythm and its hierarchic complexities. In fact, the oneness and unity between speech and body motion is truly awesome.

Theta brainwaves pulse at rates from about 240 to 420 per minute. This corresponds with up-tempo musics that move faster than human perceptual capacities for identifying each individual pulse as a distinct identity. The speed of alpha waves ranges from about 480 to 780 per minute, which are tempos reaching toward the very fastest physically playable time sequences and beyond the limits for cortically processing a pulse as such. Beta waves move at rates from about 960 to 1860 beats per minute, which is up to just below the minimum rate of perceptible pitch. Hall notes that:

> The definition of the self is deeply embedded in the rhythmic synchronic process. This is because rhythm is inherent in organization, and therefore has a basic design function in the organization of the personality. Rhythm cannot be separated from process and structure; in fact one can question whether there is such a thing as an eventless rhythm. Rhythmic patterns may turn out to be one of the most important basic personality traits that differentiate one human being from the next. All human rhythms begin in the center of the self, that is with self-synchrony.
>
> ... No matter where one looks on the face of this earth, wherever there are people, they can be observed syncing when music is played. There is a popular misconception

> about music. Because there is a beat to music, the generally accepted belief is that the rhythm originates in the music, not that music is a highly specialized releaser of rhythms already in the individual. ... Music can also be viewed as a rather remarkable extension of the(se) rhythms.

Master percussionist Milford Graves has researched the pulses of the literal, individual human heart as a primary locus of human rhythm and as a musical resource. A seasoned practitioner of acupuncture, herbalism and martial arts already well versed in Nigerian, Haitian and Cuban drum languages, Graves recognized that particular wisdoms concerning the interaction of musical time with heart rhythms had already been empirically worked out by musicians centuries before without the benefit of experimental analysis and theory. He began recording heartbeats to inquire into their peculiar musicality to discover that a healthy heartbeat is actually a syncopated and polyrhythmic one, that amid the more evident primary pulses are more temporally irregular concurrent rhythmic pulses that, interestingly enough, most resemble the motion of free jazz.

One of the most dangerously vulnerable of heartbeats is one that pulses at the equidistant pace of clone time, stopwatch time, technical time. What it indicates is that the heart is no longer responding to its environment. It's lost touch and has become unable to respond to the variable, complex, shifting nature of actual events.

If a sound might seem without rhythm, its listener will certainly bring some and/or discover some. If human interaction is intrinsically rhythmic, why wouldn't musical interaction be rhythmic? And, why would music, like rhythm, *not* be biological, responsorial, dialogical and communicative?

Better Behaved Metrics

A key divergence between monological and dialogical dispositions toward time is in their handling of rhythm. In both, rhythm directs attention to quantity, measure, proportion, placement, sequence, emphasis, anticipation, magnetism, gravity, velocity, density, probability, predictability and shape. Monological applications tend to treat these primarily as dimensional components of a sonorous object being displayed. And while this may be no less a practical concern in dialogical contexts, these same rhythmic components also constitute interface and reference, posing intersections for structural communication and providing episodes of resistance against which to further decide. Dialogical rhythm facilitates association and interconnection, whether through divergence or convergence. It's a call listening for response. Dialogical rhythm is intended to start something, to make something happen, to provoke fresh input and change, whereas monological objects tend to examine rhythm more as an illustrational device.

This might be easiest to notice in monological music where rhythm is given more design weight than elsewhere, as is the case with the musical tendency referred to as Minimalism, initiated by such composers as Terry Riley, Steve Reich, David Borden and Phillip Glass. These composers were much less circumspect about their debts to Afrological musics and other musics outside a pan-European inheritance. The foreground incorporation of looping rhythmic patterns with subtle, gradual transformations is unequivocally African and has no precedent whatsoever in Euroclassical practice. Riley has jazz experience and isn't afraid of improvisation. Reich studied in Ghana and has been unapologetic in his admiration for John Coltrane's music.

But the intentions are radically different. The surface of most of Reich's music is replete with unoffensively pretty, cleanly tempered pitch intervals, often of a pentatonic or modal flavor, so much so that one might be tempted to hear it as sort of "Debussy does Africa," except that that would be an insult to Debussy, who was never limp or decorative in his explorations of sound's potential sensuosities. Although Reich's adopted sonorities might appeal to high art aspiring listeners more comfortable with The Doors' *Light My Fire* vamp tribute to Trane's *My Favorite Things* than to the perhaps unsettling Black Utopia dreamed by Coltrane, Reich's shopping-mall-bland palette is adroitly intended to direct listener attention to incremental development and evolution within the music's sound body, which he accomplishes with great care, nuance and clarity.

The minimalist composers have constructed intricate and imaginative sonic imagery that couldn't be achieved any other way (and often quite highly demanding of its performers), which is genuinely to their credit and well worth taking seriously, but they nevertheless continue a tradition of crafting precious objects for careful display within safely insulated vitrines. Rhythm, the shape and pattern of motion itself, has been, after centuries of religious and intellectual, suspicion, granted a respectable seat at the Eurological table, but it's politely asked *not* to motivate.

Hyperrhythms in Waiting

Composer Conlon Nancarrow worked as a jazz trumpeter before joining the Abraham Lincoln brigade to fight totalitarian fascists during the Spanish Civil War. Disgusted with later being stigmatized for this contribution by his own government in the "land of the free," he renounced his U.S. citizenship and lived the rest of his life in Mexico City. There, he came upon the notion of manually punching player piano rolls to design and sound his own constructions well before the technical options of computer and synthesizer generated sound would become available. Although unable to deliver the full pianoforte nuance of the human hand, the piano roll was unrestricted by number of fingers or reach and could sound humanly impossible agglomerations of what a piano keyboard could deliver, an opportunity that prompted his compositional imagination to probe beyond the reasonable or ordinarily practical.

His earliest works for this medium show his affection, respect and understanding toward U.S. African music as they extrapolate from a percussive foundation in boogie-woogie pianism and expand upon polyrhythmic principles of contrasting simultaneous multiple tempo strata further integrated with the sound mirroring potentials of canonic reflection and refraction. His designs progress from one to another with contagious what-if experimentation, relentlessly pushing the envelope beyond what anyone could play and what anyone had heard. Nancarrow's utopian soniverse dreams toward a musical world that could happen in practice but, having been developed in the isolation of exile, leaves, at least for starters, some deeply thought through and viscerally impressive promises of what might be assayed.

Monological scholarship of Nancarrow's work seems most drawn to its mathematical complexity, with rhythm evaluated primarily as a sophisticated abstract intellectual quantity. One important compositional analyst doesn't even appear to find it necessary to find out, much less know, about concurrent, and not entirely unrelated, Afrological rhythmic investigations. Pyrotechnic displays of architectonic numerical virtuosity seem enough to justify not even considering dialogical designs and implications.

Nancarrow wasn't at all constructing sound bodies just to show off, but there are compositional questions this remarkable sound sculpture format isn't able to pursue. Designs to be sounded through a remote device — whether that be player piano, tape or amplified computer — doesn't deal with the same structural challenges that successfully transferring compositional information to and through interpretive performers does. And dialogical structures are indigenously far more complex than both of these situations before either a single idea has entered the exchange or a first sound has emerged.

Inhabited Rhythm

Rhythms are more than pattern. They *happen*. Being location and moment specific, they have to be embodied. In fact, following on Condon' and Hall's observations, rhythm can't be meaningfully separated from the reality of emergent bodily experience and existence. They can't be assimilated within the limits of simplified, two dimensional abstractions or concepts. They have also to be felt, in some way understood, lived through and acted out. They have to be communicable, not only recognizable by a dialogical actor, but they have to be clearly enough articulated to reach other composers within an ensemble. They have to function multidimensionally, not only as numerically intriguing configurations, but as motion code, encapsulations of gradations of movement, proprioceptive redistributions, internal sensation, reactive templates. Design complexity for its own sake would, in this context, be most liable to yield the illustrational dryness of a bureaucratic missive. To put it almost tautologically, dialogical rhythmic design has to *motivate*. Its momentum has to (as Butch Morris has characterized the interactive essence of swing) spontaneously ignite, combust and propel.

This isn't to say that rhythm must be metrically coordinated. Breath or interaction can reference rhythmic motion as effectively. What matters are the communicative interconnections that rhythm both characterizes and facilitates.

Neuroscientist António Damásio has so rewoven and repaired possible notions of brain-body intercommunication that it's hard any more to insist on a practical separation of the two (one of his best known books is entitled, somewhat unsurprisingly, *Descartes' Error*). Well beyond the obvious nutritional dependency of brains on the organisms within which they function, Damásio followed the implications of damage to various areas of the brain to a discovery that what's called rational thought is actually unsustainable without the orientation provided by emotion. Emotion confirms value, which then undergirds and directs thinking in setting priorities and maintaining focus. He describes how thinking plays out ideas and possible eventualities in the "theater of the body," that one calls upon actual bodily sensations (in other words, *feeling*) while weighing thought.

Within a still wider arc, this same human rationality "must be seen as a form and derivative of a broader 'mentality,' or subjectivity, in nature as a whole," as politcal philosopher Murray Bookchin has put it in his *Ecology of Freedom*. Onöndowa'ga:' scholar John Mohawk also notes that Haudenosaunee understandings regard humans as the only ones around even capable of *ir*-rationality, an awareness that can help keep the allegations and practices of technocratic abstraction, or of any imperialism of instrumentality (whether in music or elsewhere), somewhat more within sane perspective.

Rhythm no less plays the theater of bodily consciousness, and its languages can be recognized as auditory parallels to the sculptor's. Neither meaningfully drifts very far from the tactile, the actual, the kinetic and the concretely lived, nor can rhythm be sensibly distanced from personhood and therefore from human and compositional interaction. "Sounds in themselves" may or may not need rhythm, but rhythm, without a doubt, biologizes and humanizes sound.

20

Hearing

"You listen to music, but you *hear* yo mama." One can turn a radio or a recording on or off, but an actual person isn't going to respond, settle or participate all *that* schematically.

To listen reaches out, attends — which means *to be there*. It focuses, chooses, waits, takes in. Peripheral hearing might register a few sounds "out there" — some vibrations that happen to be stirring the ear follicles. Listening, however, is optional. It's a *choice*.

One may listen but still not *hear*. But, without listening, one won't ever *hear*.

To *hear* is not necessarily to agree, but it *is* to recognize, to acknowledge, even more so to comprehend, to project, to imagine and dream, to associate and interconnect, perhaps to be changed somehow, to further understand *where* and *who* a sound is coming from, maybe even *why*, and possibly *how*.

Hearing reaches beyond the sound behind the sound maybe even before the sound, and whatever "in the beginnings" had to have been way way way before the sound. Hearing listens even farther past that to the sounds that haven't yet found a way, or a place, to happen. Hearing becomes magnetized and can slow gestate the yet unheard.

Hearing frames, contextualizes, interprets. No two angles resound the same. No two people hear exactly alike. And, if you don't *hear* it, well, maybe you just don't get it. Maybe it's just not for you. But, then sometimes, sometimes much, or even much much later, you *do* find a way to *hear*.

Or, perhaps a sound has finally found *you*, maybe even found some way to *hear* you, too. One musician might never fully *hear* another unless they actually get to *play* together, to earwitness *from the inside* the distinctive curves and frequencies of response and initiative that cradle the sounds. And, sometimes, to *hear* might even mean to get all the way over to the other side of someones else's ears.

Cetaceans — whales, dolphins, porpoises — listen with sonar. They send out sounds and listen to what reverberations sound back. They can *hear* another body's innards, the composition, the skeleton, the tensions that shape muscle and propulsion, the nervous system's pique.

The sound of a voice draws a listener deep into the body of another, the ever so light traces of air just recently inside someone else's lungs sculpted through modulations of diaphragm, rib cage, pharynx, nasal cavities, teeth, tongue, lips, passageways so kin with the familiars of one's own internal topography that it might likewise wax projectable, perceptible, inhabitable. And, one can no less *hear* without literally hearing oneself: the sounds of skull, blood flow, nerve buzz, breath, the ways one oneself composes.

Hearing is empathy that fulfills the reach of listening.

21

& Some
Coda
Considerations

It would be nice to be "right," but don't count on it. It's impossible to please everybody all the time about everything. No claims to any sort of normative "universality" are being entertained despite whatever searches for common threads might happen to soak through. This is no Encyclopedia Panopticon. The perspectives inclining these wonderings have developed through specific lived experiences of the sonic creoles of occupied Turtle Island, and within New York City in particular (and from within some fairly marginally positioned circles of activity inside that) during a few decades before and since the millennium. New York has never been the whole world, and this is neither all time nor any time. The lines of thought emergent here instead relate and respond to specific experiences, people I've gotten to know, worked with, seen in action, conversed with, overheard, maybe disagreed with, books I may have come across, performances witnessed, all somewhat occluded by the shadows of all those whom I'd wished I'd known to those I'll never hear of, of books and whatever else there is yet to discover. Any location, any position, is unavoidably blindsided amid opacities. Plenty has therefore been left out or missed, or mislaid, lost, bypassed, forgotten, misunderstood, or not even thought of, much less heard or heard of. In other words, there's a point of view (which is itself also a work in progress), only one particular juncture among a necessary diversity of differences. Most contradictions encountered here are deliberate. Think about how a view changes as one rotates a landscape or a sculpture. And quite a bit of what's ordinarily thought of as "music" isn't even addressed here. Hardly any attention has been directed toward musical sound's accompaniment functions in cinema, video, live theater, much concert dance and whatever other multimedia formulations where sound might contribute. The ambiguity of song is likewise deliberately left off the radar. The inflections of spoken language are themselves, of course, absolutely musical, as are the sonic transformations of language by such artists as Billie Holiday. Poetry especially pitches toward song — and has for likely as long as humans have voiced. But, a threshold is nevertheless crossed where linguistic images push the gratuitous difficulty of the ear off to the side for other, even more synesthetic projections, where a sound body no longer speaks, or holds up, on its own without words being "understood," where musical sound becomes valued primarily as background ambience. Nor does this exploration especially concern "style," what distinguishes "good" or "bad" or "better" musics, or conventional notions of "musical structure" (which is usually just another way of saying "sound design"). If anything, the reach of this particular thinking-through-out-loud embedded in paper and ink has been toward a recognition of sound design's interdependence with the compositional structures of how people listen, imagine, decide, communicate and coordinate, that all of this *together* distinguishes a music's structure (which is not to exclude or deny however sound might musick among birds, whales, tree limbs or cicadas, these musics being theirs to decide). None of this is "objectively" disinterested (as if that could, in any way, be either possible or honest). Accepting that all this matters, while continually testing experience generated opinion, has propelled this along with the triple drivers of curiosity, love (if not, romance) and dissatisfaction.

Thelonious Monk, whose status as innovator is comparable to that of Christian, Gillespie and Parker, is also in a sense a very special descendant of the downhome honky-tonk player who likes to sit alone in the empty ballroom and play around with unconventional chord combinations and rhythms for his own private enjoyment. There is something of the empty ballroom étude in almost all of Monk's compositions.

— Albert Murray
Stomping the Blues

Related Reading

People may often think by themselves, but nobody thinks alone. The following listing of books and authors include those who, for me, have demonstrated ways to write, those whose concepts have directly fed into and influenced my own, those whom I've come across who have likewise delved into the formative roles of interaction in music, as well as those valued antagonistic cooperators, whose less than sympathetic perspectives have helped me to sharpen my own. The rest have provided sources for quotations and paraphrase found throughout this book. All of it has been worthwhile and stimulating reading for me and might also be of interest for you.

Christophe Cox (editor)
Audio Culture: Readings in Modern Music (Bloomsbury Academic, 2004)

Albert Murray
The Hero and the Blues (University of Missouri Press, 1973)
The Omni-Americans: Some Alternatives to the Folklore of White Supremacy (DaCapo, 1990)
Stomping the Blues (McGraw Hill, 1976)

Robert Farris Thompson
Aesthetic of the Cool: Afro-Atlantic Art and Music (Periscope Publishing, 2011)
African Art in Motion (University of California Press, 1974)
Flash of the Spirit: African and Afro-American Art and Philosophy (Random House,1983)
Tango: An Art History of Love (Pantheon Books, 2005)

James Baldwin
The Price of the Ticket: Collected Non-Fiction 1948-1985 (St. Martin's/Mabek, 1985)

Gaston Bachillard
The Poetics of Space (Beacon, 1994)

John Miller Chernoff
African Rhythm and African Sensibility: Aesthetics and Social Action in African Musical Idioms (University of Chicago, 1979)

David Abram
*The Spell of the Sensuous:
Perception and Language in a More-than-Human World,* (Pantheon, 1996)

António Damásio
Descarte's Error: Emotion, Reason, and the Human Brain (Penguin Books, 2005)

Edward T. Hall
The Dance of Life: The Other Dimension of Time (Penguin Books, 1984)

LeRoi Jones/Amiri Baraka
Blues People (William Morrow, 1963)
Black Music (William Morrow, 1969)

Bruno Latour
We Have Never Been Modern (Harvard University Press, 1991)
Visualization and Cognition: Drawing Things Together in
Knowledge and Society: Studies in the Sociology of Culture Past and Present, (Jai Press vol. 6, pp. 1-40)

Charles Olson
Projective Verse (1950)

Morse Peckham
Man's Rage for Chaos: Biology, Behavior & the Arts (Schocken Books, 1957)

David Borgo
Sync & Swarm: Improvising Music in a Complex Age (Bloomsbury, 2006)

George E. Lewis
Improvised Music after 1950: Afrological and Eurological Perspectives
(Black Music Research Journal, Vol 3, Columbia College Chicago Center for Black Music Research, 1983)

Lawrence D. "Butch" Morris
The Art of *Conduction:* (Karma, 2017)

Ingrid Monson
Saying Something: Jazz Improvisation and Interaction
(University of Chicago Press, *1996)*

Christopher Small
Music of the Common Tongue:
Survival and Celebration in Afro-American Music (Riverrun Press, 1987)
Musicking: The Meanings of Performing and Listening
(University Press of New England,1998)

Theodor Adorno
Philosophy of Modern Music (Continuum, 2004)

John Cage
Silence: Lectures and Writings by John Cage (M.I.T. Press, 1966),
A Year from Monday: New Lectures and Writings by John Cage
(Wesleyan University Press,1970)
John Cage (Richard Kostelanetz, Praeger, 1970)

V. Kofi Agawu
Playing with Signs: A Semiotic Interpretation of Classic Music
(Princeton University Press, 1991)

Derek Bailey
Improvisation: Its Nature and Practice in Music (DaCapo, 1993)

Walter Benjamin —
Illuminations (Harrcourt, Brace & World, 1968)

Murray Bookchin
The Ecology of Freedom: The Emergence and Dissolution of Hierarchy
(AK Press, 2005)

Jeff Chang
Can't Stop Wont Stop: A History of the Hip Hop Generation
(St. Martin's Press, 2005)

Gordon Hempton & John Grossman
One Square Inch of Silence:
One Man's Search for Natural Silence in a Noisy World (Free Press, 2009)

Don Ihde
Listening and Voice : A Phenomenology of Sound
(Ohio University Press, 1976)

Arthur Jafa
My Black Death
(in *Everything but the Burden,* ed. Greg Tate, Broadway Books, 2003)

David McNeill
Hand and Mind: What Gestures Reveal about Thought
(University of Chicago Press, 1992)

John Mohawk
Prologue to *The White Roots of Peace* (Paul A.W. Wallace)
(Chauncy Press, 1986)

Walter Pater
The Renaissance: Studies in Art and Poetry
(University of California Press, 1980)

Theodor Schwenk
Sensitive Chaos: The Creation of Flowing Forms in Water and Air
(Rudolph Steiner Press, 1996)
Water: The Element of Life (Steiner Books, 2003)

Online Supplements

Glossary of Invented or Repurposed Terms

People

https://www.arteidolia.com/arteidolia-press-ways-sounds-online-supplements/

About the Author

New York City composer, bandleader & alto saxophonist patrick brennan has pursued a contrarian and independent musical path toward evolving a distinct musical language in relation with the Blues Continuum. He formed his rhythm-section-centric ensemble *sOnic Openings* in 1979, which is an ongoing project that interfaces flexibly jointed compositional matrices with polyrhythm & collective improvisation. He has performed and recorded internationally with this and other initiatives, ranging from solo, to large formats, to collaborations with the Gnawa as well as with electro-acoustic improvisers. His published essays and reviews have engaged cinema, music, poetry and visual art.

patrickbrennansound.com

www.ingramcontent.com/pod-product-compliance
Lightning Source LLC
Chambersburg PA
CBHW020934090426
42736CB00010B/1139